HARDSCAPING

HOW TO USE STRUCTURES, PATHWAYS, PATIOS & ORNAMENTS IN YOUR GARDEN

KEITH DAVITT

Sterling Publishing Co., Inc.
New York

For my sister Bonnie,
whose achievements far exceed my own.

Garden Design, Photography, and other Credits are on page 255

Library of Congress Cataloging-in-Publication Data
Davitt, Keith.
 Hardscaping : how to use structures, pathways, patios & ornaments in your garden / Keith Davitt.
   p. cm.
  ISBN 1-4027-1876-4
 1. Landscape gardening. 2. Garden structures. I. Title.

SB473.D393 2006
717—dc22

                                                    2005024127

10 9 8 7 6 5 4 3 2 1

Published by Sterling Publishing Co., Inc.
387 Park Avenue South, New York, NY 10016
© 2006 by Keith Davitt
Distributed in Canada by Sterling Publishing
C/o Canadian Manda Group, 165 Dufferin Street
Toronto, Ontario, Canada M6K 3H6
Distributed in the United Kingdom by GMC Distribution Services,
Castle Place, 166 High Street, Lewes, East Sussex, England BN7 1XU
Distributed in Australia by Capricorn Link (Australia) Pty. Ltd.
P.O. Box 704, Windsor, NSW 2756, Australia

Printed in China
All rights reserved

Sterling ISBN-13: 978-1-4027-1876-2
          ISBN-10: 1-4027-1876-4

For information about custom editions, special sales, premium and
corporate purchases, please contact Sterling Special Sales
Department at 800-805-5489 or specialsales@sterlingpub.com.

Contents

Introduction

How many of us have found ourselves looking into the foliage and flower beds of a garden we designed and wondered why our design didn't work? The plant combinations were gorgeous, a continuum of blossoms appeared from spring through fall, and even in winter it kept our interest. But somehow, something was missing.

That something was hardscaping. Of the clients who call me, frustrated with the results of their own efforts, most have overlooked the importance of placing hard structures in the garden. Structure delineates, punctuates, ornaments, animates, adds dimensionality, and gives balance and focus—and a garden is not complete without it.

Structures, or hardscape, can be light or heavy, formal or informal, small or large, vertical or horizontal, natural or man-made. What sort of structure and how much is appropriate for your garden will depend on the garden itself and on your tastes and needs. The choices include arbors, paving, or walls of stone, brick, or wood. You can use fountains, birdbaths, streams, or pools. Decks, benches, lattice, and pergolas also provide structure, as do pots, planters, a grouping of stones, and even a single piece of sculpture. These elements stand out from, contrast with, and give balance to the plantings and help to create a definition of space and invoke a sense of place.

Hardscape elements can serve both functional and aesthetic purposes at the same time. Retaining walls, for example, are superb structural elements, as they create planting spaces, provide dimensionality, and give the garden strength. Arbors can both separate and join two garden "rooms," and give the garden vertical structure while doing so. Structures can be used to frame a garden or to delineate spaces within it. Structure can serve simply as ornamentation, or be used to support plants, generate a sense of motion, or give the eye a solid element upon which to rest.

Finally, structure provides permanence. A garden consisting only of plants tends to vanish with time. The space remains, but the individual elements that made that space special often succumb to eras of neglect and the indifference of time. Structure helps a garden to endure, particularly if structural elements are used not only within the garden but also to define and delineate the space.

The purpose of this book is to show the importance of structures. We will look at the various functions they perform and how they can be incorporated into the landscape. Each chapter starts by introducing the reader to the design principles involved.

We will examine specific gardens and see how their structural elements turn them into livable, beautiful spaces. Although each garden is used to exemplify one function of structure in particular, each garden also demonstrates several other uses and effects of structure. These other functions are pointed out for each garden.

Some of the gardens presented on these pages are of my own design, but many more are gardens from various other designers across the United States and Europe. For the most part, I have chosen gardens I find particularly appealing and that demonstrate well the principles I am attempting to convey.

This book is intended for anyone interested in designing gardens. You needn't be a beginner to benefit from the analysis of hardscape features found in the wide range of outdoor settings presented here. I have yet to pick up a garden design book or hear a colleague speak without learning valuable information myself.

As Fawn Hayes Bell, an award-winning landscape architect, said at a symposium we both conducted at the Denver Botanic Gardens recently, understanding *why* we are affected in a particular way by some design element introduces us to a design principle. We then can choose how we will employ that principle or go beyond it, seeking new solutions.

Having the knowledge behind design principles equips us for those times and situations in which inspiration fails to supply us with a design that satisfies. If we know that dimensionality, for example, is an important ingredient in landscape and garden design, we might examine a design over which we are struggling to see if this principle might be brought to bear. Such is the case with the concept of balance, the power of focal points, and so forth.

It's fine to design by instinct or some quality of emotional cognition. Most of us do. But knowing, intellectually, the principles behind successful designs can only assist us in furthering our comprehension and leading us to greater achievements in the pursuit of creating beautiful gardens.

—Keith Davitt
Cambridge, New York

CHAPTER 1

Structure & Balance

Every garden lacking some form of structural component also lacks balance. This is simply because when the eye has only foliage and blossoms to take in, with no solid elements upon which to rest, it becomes weary and looks around for something more tangible upon which to settle. A great deal of foliage or even an abundance of blossoms without the counterpoint of a structural element will please us, but briefly; in contrast, a garden composed of both softscape and hardscape continually refreshes the eye, allowing a prolonged enjoyment of each element and combination of elements.

I first became aware of this phenomenon when visiting gardens in Jamaica. I was surprised to find myself disturbed by the sight of gardens of incredible lushness everywhere I went. The gardens were beautiful but not satisfying. Then I was shown another luxuriant garden with a large ceramic sculpture embedded within it, and the relief and satisfaction was profound. I realized this was what the other gardens were missing. All that lushness cried out for something solid.

The easiest way to experience the problem of imbalance and its resolution is to find a planting containing no structure and place something solid within it. If you have a lushly planted perennial bed or a shrub border, for example, try placing an ornamental pot, a sculpture, or even a large stone or piece of wood within it and see how it improves. Or take a very small planted area, such as a ground-cover bed, and set something solid within it. Both the plants as well as the hard element will be seen to greater advantage. Even well-planned and planted gardens will benefit from the addition of structural components. Many a beautiful perennial bed would be a considerably more satisfying composition with some appropriate solid element added to it.

Here, we focus on the principle of balance in order to establish its importance in all garden creations. We will first look at simple structures placed within planting beds and then move on to larger settings in which the principle of balance involves entire expanses.

Simple Balance

This series of garden scenes demonstrates the dramatic improvement simple structures can provide to lush plantings. Each photograph includes a modified image in which the structure was replaced digitally by plants. The purpose here is to show the simplest use of structures and to demonstrate how effective simple structures can be when placed in proximity to an abundance of foliage and flowers.

This first image **(1-1)** is a digitally modified version of image **1-2**, showing the same garden with plants in place of the ceramic pot. The garden without the pot is certainly pretty, but how long can you look at it with interest? Image **1-2**, however, invites us back again and again to enjoy this very pretty and satisfying scene.

Similar principles apply with gardens three through six **(1-3** through **1-10).** The solid structures in each of these scenes imbue the gardens with a vitality otherwise lacking. The hardscape elements make the gardens "pop"—they give them life. They invite a prolonged enjoyment of the gardens they occupy, giving us a sense of satisfaction lacking when they are removed. But what exactly is it about these objects that does this?

First, it is the *forms* themselves. Plants are very complex in structure, as anyone who has tried to draw them knows, whereas these hardscape components— the pot in the first garden, the birdbaths in gardens two, three, and four, and the rock in the fourth garden—are simple forms that are easily perceived. We love the abundant variety of the plantings, but we need the solid and simple forms to return to before visually venturing out across the garden again. The simplicity of the hardscape forms balances with the complexity of the plant forms, refreshing our vision and thereby allowing us to have a prolonged enjoyment of the garden.

> ## A FEW THOUGHTS ON
> ### The Power of Contrast
> The greater the impact that a structural element provides, the fewer such elements are necessary, as is evident in **1-2.** The ceramic pot is quite enough, with its shiny surface and simple, pleasing form. But note that it is not only the contrasts of form, texture, and color that provide this impact, but also the harmony with the blue Salvia. When both harmony and contrasts are present within a single composition, our most emphatic response is elicited.

1-1 This is the same scene as shown in 1-2 with the pot removed digitally. Notice how less interesting and engaging the scene is.

1-2 The ceramic pot is integral to the beauty of this garden. The pot anchors the plants and provides a dramatic contrast in form and texture. In color, it contrasts nicely with the pink Oriental poppy and the red hollyhocks, while harmonizing with the Salvia.

1-3 The same scene as in 1-4 with the birdbath removed digitally. Note the lack of anywhere for the eye to rest before resuming an enjoyment of the flowers and foliage.

1-4 A single hardscape element brings balance to the abundant planting and allows the eye to be refreshed by the garden's simplicity.

As garden two **(1-4),** with its clipped box and juniper shrubs, shows, plants can have definite forms. Such plants often are used for just this purpose of balancing with the relative formlessness of more wayward plants. Yet even distinctly formed plants still consist of foliage, and this brings us to the next point.

In addition to their form, hardscape components have a *textural quality* and *solidity* that contribute to the balancing act they perform in the garden. Almost every plant is a complexity of relatively soft surfaces perceived as an almost infinite display of points of light. The hardscape components, with their solid *touchableness,* provide relief from the ineffable delicacy and complexity of the foliage and flowers. This balance, provided by the textural quality of a solid structure, allows us to plunge back into the garden with renewed appreciation.

Scale/Proportion

In scale, the blue pot in the first garden **(1-2)** is perfect, and this is why: The abundant flowers could use a considerable degree of structure. Yet because this pot appears so much more massive than most glazed terra-cotta pots we are accustomed to seeing, it has the impact of a larger pot and this makes it seem quite ample for its setting. In addition, the pot's strong contrast with the surrounding plants makes it appear more dominant in the garden. With its hard, shiny surface and distinctively simple form, it stands out from the lush planting. It also creates a contrast in color. While it harmonizes nicely with the blue Salvia, it contrasts with the pink poppies and the red hollyhock.

The birdbath in the second garden **(1-4)** also works well in terms of scale and for similar reasons. Because the birdbath contrasts so strongly with the plants surrounding it, though they are very abundant, it is sufficient. It might have been tempting to use a larger structure here, but any more than this in this setting would draw attention from the beautiful plants, and that is not its purpose.

Style

The way the hardscape element contributes to the style of the garden is as important as its scale within the setting. The first garden, with its blue pot and array of perennials, is in the English cottage garden tradition in that it is lush, colorful, and casual. The pot and plants harmonize nicely in creating this effect.

The second garden has more of an elegant feel to it, owing to the formal birdbath, the clipped shrubs, and the more carefully arranged perennials and annuals. The larger Hosta and smaller Coleus in the foreground form a splendid foliar harmony/contrast relationship. Behind them are white Nicotiana to the left, orange-red fibrous Begonia, and yellow pansies. Above are various lilies, a Fuchsia, and red Geraniums.

1-5 The same scene as in 1-6 without the birdbath, but it fails to hold our interest or to satisfy.

1-6 The birdbath here harmonizes in color with the lush bed of snow-in-summer, while providing a much-needed balance of texture and form.

1-7 A pretty scene composed entirely of foliage and flowers with almost no structural elements. The Iris do provide a vertical accent serving nearly the same function as a structure, but as pretty a scene as this is, we soon lose interest in it. Now regard image 1-8 with the birdbath in place.

1-8 This is the same garden scene as in 1-7 with the structures in place. It is much more satisfying, as it allows the eye to traverse from softscape to hardscape and back again, with pleasure.

1-9 The same scene as in 1-10, but lacking the balancing hard element of the stone.

1-10 Here, simple stones help balance with the sea of Sedum acre, out of which rise fernleaf yarrow (*Achillea filipendulina* 'Moonshine') and Dianthus x.

A FEW THOUGHTS ON
Natural versus Man-Made

Generally, man-made elements such as the pot, the wood vine towers, and the stone birdbaths will create more dramatic contrasts with the plants than will natural components like the rocks in **1-11.** This is because we often see stones and plants in harmony in nature—we are used to finding them together—and because stones are more amorphous and less formal, than fabricated structures, as are plants. Natural components and plants complement each other through form and texture, while displaying a subtle harmony **(1-12).**

1-11 Here, stones are embedded in Sedum acre with the glossy-leafed Bergenia behind and lamb's ears (*Stachys byzantina*) to the left.

1-12 Plant life grows on the stones, harmonizing with the surrounding planting, yet still providing the balance in form and texture.

Additional Hardscape Functions

These structures also add *dimension,* and they serve as *focal point*s. For more details on these functions, see Chapters 2 and 5, respectively.

Application

    Virtually any fairly dense planting, be it a shrub border, a perennial border, or a mixed border, will benefit from the inclusion of simple structures. These solid elements will provide a balance and contrast to the abundant foliage, bringing out the beauty of the garden.

Planting

1-2: Pink Oriental poppy (*Papaver orientalis*), red hollyhocks (*Alcea rosea*), blue Salvia (*Salvia* x)

1-4: Hosta, Coleus, Begonia, pansy, lily, Chamaecyparis, Fucshia

1-6: Snow-in-summer (*Cerastium tomentosum*)

1-8: Iris, peony, *Geranium* 'Johnson's Blue,' *Alchemilla mollis*

1-10: Sedum, Dianthus, Achillea

1-11: Sedum, Stachys, Bergenia, Dianthus, Achillea

Spatial Balance

The previous gardens demonstrated the concept of balance and harmony-within a particular setting. In these next two gardens, we explore the concept of creating harmony between hard and soft spaces such that neither dominates the other within the entire framework of the garden **(1-13)**.

On a larger scale, hardscape can be used to create balance within the garden as a spatial whole, as this garden so beautifully demonstrates. The garden in **1-13** is a handsome composition of paved and green spaces in perfect balance. The textures and colors create balance through contrast, while the volumes are balanced through their similarity. The planted pots distributed about the hardscape area and the paving inset in the lawn serve to unite the two areas, helping to achieve that so desirable quality of *unity with diversity*. At the same time, they deepen the expression of balance. Not only does the hard area balance with the softscape, but within each area there is balance.

Scale/Proportion

Scale here is important. Were either of the two areas made much larger, the other would have seemed too small and thus disappointing. If either area had been made smaller, the massive border planting would have dwarfed it. We would feel the imbalance, and the garden simply would not have been what it could be and is.

Style

Both the hardscape and softscape areas are harmonious in their simple geometry. The softscape has been given a central axis, accentuated by the diamond paving, the diagonal hedges, and the diagonal lines and focal point at the end, while the hardscape is offset to the right. This sets up a dynamic that contributes

A FEW THOUGHTS ON
Unity & Diversity

Most gardeners want more plants than they know what to do with, more ornaments than there seem to be a place for—more elements of interest. In short, we want diversity. But diversity can be a fast road to chaos—unless measures are taken to create unity. One method for creating unity with diversity is to repeat the use of distinctive materials throughout the garden. Variegated plants are excellent for this purpose, as are bold-leafed or spiky plants. In this garden, embedding pavement in the lawn and repeating similar plant combinations in the softscape area, on the patio, has this effect.

1-13 A beautiful balance between hard- and softscape.

1-14 The dramatic foliage of New Zealand flax and *Cordyline australis* and a focal point draw our vision to the rear of the garden, uniting front with back.

to the energy of the garden. The overall effect is a contemporary feel with formal elements.

Additional Hardscape Functions

This garden could have been used to demonstrate creating *outdoor-living* areas with structures, it has elements of *ornamentation* (note the scalloped birdbath in the left corner of the patio), and it possesses a fairly effective *focal point* (the orange ball at the extreme end of the garden) **(1-14).**

Application

Many an urban yard would benefit from this sort of open division by the use of contrasting surfaces (lawn and stone). It is so much more interesting than having just lawn, and an area this size all in paving, even with ample flowerbeds, would be too much hardscape.

Planting

Phormium tenax 'Purpurea,' Cordyline australis, Hosta, ferns, Pieris.

A Formal Lawn
Between Two Pavings

The garden shown in **1-15** seems at first glance to be slightly unbalanced, with too large a lawn area dominating the paved area, until we notice the paved area to the very rear of the garden and discover a perfect equilibrium of hard- and softscape. It would have been a pleasant garden without the small paving to the rear, but with it the garden seems nearly perfect.

From the sunken outdoor-living area, the rear paving would not be missed **(1-16).** Looking back from the rear of the garden **(1-17),** however, we see there is a veranda with double French doors. The view from there is important, as a balanced composition is always a better, more satisfying choice.

Scale/Proportion

The proportions here are gorgeous, not only in the relationship of hard- and softscape but also in the individual areas and the gradual ascent from one area to another. Nothing overpowers anything—everything exists comfortably within itself, in relation to the elements around it and in relation to the whole.

Style

Although this is a formal arrangement and on the whole symmetrical, there is not a slavish attachment to symmetry. Note the off-place pot here and there and particularly the planting arrangement in the outer garden. There is no attempt at symmetry, yet this garden is nicely balanced with, for example, the purple-leafed smoke bush (*Cotinus coggygria 'Purpureus'*) on the far left, the silver-leafed autumn olive (*Eleagnus umbellata*) on the near right, and the whitish pagoda dog-wood (*Cornus controversa*) on the near left.

Both the hardscape and softscape areas are in harmony, in that each is a fairly sophisticated design. This enhances the balancing act taking place in the garden with the cross-axis hardscape area contrasting nicely with the oval lawn and the curving planting beds. The repetition of paving materials and the focal point in

1-15 The softscape is balanced by hardscape at either end of the garden.

1-16 Note the abundant structures ornamenting the garden. Clipped boxwood accentuate the formal aspects of the garden, while a host of less structured plants (Cares, Festuca, *Rosa* x 'Golden Showers') soften the setting and make it relaxing.

the rear of the garden serve to connect the background to the front, unifying the garden while creating a sense of place.

Additional Hardscape Functions

This garden could also be used to demonstrate the effectiveness of hardscape as adding *ornamentation* **(1-16),** bringing about a *division of space,* and creating a *focal point.*

Application

All too often, gardens with considerable potential are treated as a single space and not developed into a more complex combination of spaces, each with its own look and purposes. Even small gardens can be greatly enhanced through this practice of creating different spaces. As we see in these two gardens, combining a hardscape area with planting areas in a unified composition can be considerably more satisfying than merely cultivating a lawn with plants.

Planting

Boxwood (*Buxus*), Carex, Festuca, *Rosa* x 'Golden Showers,' Syringa, *'Variegatus,' Eleagnus angustifolius*, smoke bush (*Cotinus coggygria 'Purpureus'*), silver-leafed autumn olive (*Eleagnus umbellata*), pagoda dogwood (*Cornus controversa*).

1-17 Balance, from the view of the veranda, is an important element of the overall design. At this end of the garden, clipped boxwood add the formal touch while variegated Hosta, Aconitum, and Helleborus tone down the formality.

Balancing the World

A final consideration related to the concept of using structure to create balance is the notion of balancing with the larger outside world. In many places, of course, our gardens are not experienced in relation to the larger world. Suburban gardens, for example, are generally fairly contiguous, with one running into the next. We don't see much distinction between them, and they don't have much connection with the outside world. In many rural settings, however, a garden is perceived as abiding within the countryside surrounding it. In this instance, creating a well-defined space balanced against the outer world provides a feeling of well-being and security.

These next several images **(1-18, 1-19,** and **1-20)** show a formally laid out and very well defined garden surrounded by a natural landscape. Each of the garden beds contains its own structural element, balancing with the abundant foliage and flowers. The lattice fencing provides a structural framework for the entire garden, giving it strict definition. We appreciate, by contrast, the civilized and civilizing quality of this formal garden in the context of the far larger landscape of the countryside, easily visible just beyond its borders. The garden provides a counterpoint, and one that we can palpably appreciate, to the unknown world beyond.

Scale/Proportion

In relation to the surrounding world, this garden could be made to be huge and not be out of scale, but it would then be out of scale with the home. If it were made considerably smaller, it would seem too small and the surrounding landscape would appear overpowering. Had the approach of emulating the surrounding landscape been taken and natural-looking gardens created, scale would have been far less critical. As it is, this formal garden is about the width of the home and comfortably occupies its allotted space. Within the garden, everything seems fairly well scaled, though, if we want to get really picky, the vine towers look a little tall without the vines and the low stone planters might be more satisfying if slightly taller.

1-18 Ornamental structures within the garden balance the abundant plantings.

A FEW THOUGHTS ON
Relating to the World Beyond

One approach to making a garden that balances against a very rural setting is to create its opposite on an adequately large scale, as this garden demonstrates. Another contrasting, and very satisfying method of achieving harmony in relation to the larger surrounding landscape is to create a garden in which the outside world is reflected in the immediate garden areas. This, however, requires that the garden areas be more natural, particularly in planting schemes and building materials, and would generally preclude creating formal gardens.

This homeowner's tastes tend toward the formal, so he has chosen the first approach. This method allows us to cultivate a formal garden with a particular, wide range of plants, while creating a balance against the landscape beyond. If, on the other hand, you want to bring the feeling of the surrounding countryside into your garden, the second approach is the one to follow. You can use appropriate plants, stones, and such that will reflect the surrounding country, and frame and capture views, binding your gardens with the outside world.

1-19 Here, the formal garden balances with the surrounding countryside rather than being absorbed within it.

1-20 A pergola serves as a focal point and offers a destination and a place of rest.

Style

Were ornamentation and formal beauty not the objective, any well-organized space would have created a pleasant balance with the surrounding countryside, as the vegetable garden, with its orderly arrangement, demonstrates **(1-21)**. But they were, primarily because the interior of the house is laid out on this axial arrangement and the garden is centered on it. Its classical formality is softened by the cheerful planting, and its balanced symmetry is mitigated by the variety of species.

Additional Hardscape Functions

Although the primary role of structure in this garden is to provide balance within the garden and between the garden and the surrounding countryside, there are other factors at work as well. The lattice fence provides a light frame to the garden, giving the pleasant sense of *delineation*, and at the far end of the allée, a pergola awaits, offering *privacy*. Both of these structures are designed in the same

1-21 A garden house and orderly vegetable garden balance with the natural landscape beyond.

style as the vine towers, thus contributing to the quality of unity in the garden. This garden could have been used to demonstrate structure as adding *ornamentation*, *dimensionality*, and *focal points*, and in fact we will see portions of this garden demonstrating such functions in other chapters.

Application

Gardens in rural areas can benefit from such a treatment of creating a more ordered and contained world amidst the wilder world beyond. Urban gardens, however, need this sort of balance too, especially where the city encroaches and views and sounds of it are inescapable.

Planting

Geranium 'Johnson's blue,' *Geranium sanguineum*, peonies, Siberian Iris, Japanese Iris, Hemerocallis, Astilbe, Delphinium, *Silphium perfoliatum*.

A FEW THOUGHTS ON
Frame & Focus

A picture frame will focus our attention on the picture as well as enhance the picture and possibly add another element of interest. A frame in a garden is an underutilized device that similarly brings focus and added interest to a garden. In the image of the rock garden, above, the stone border separating the rock garden planting from the lawn focuses our concentration on the rock garden as if to say, "Look here, this is worth your attention." A fence, as this formal garden shows, can do the same.

Tuteur

Although a relatively simple structure, the vine tower, or *tuteur* (tutor), does require some skill in woodworking to be built properly. These structures can be any size and come in a variety of shapes, but generally they have the shape of a pyramid **(1-22).** Therefore, the tops and bottoms of the legs and the ends of the pieces that connect the legs must be cut at a consistent angle.

It is easiest to lay out two legs on a workbench to the desired angle. Determine a perpendicular centerline between the two legs, and place each leg the same distance at the top from the centerline and the same (but wider) distance at the bottom. A line exactly perpendicular to the centerline, laid across the legs, will give the angle for cutting the bottoms and tops of the legs and the ends of the connecting braces and top brace.

Once the legs (1) and the braces (2 and 3) have been cut, they are assembled by screwing the legs to the connecting braces with the braces between the legs. The screws are countersunk into the wood, and the indentation is filled with wood putty and sanded.

For the crown support (4), cut a square large enough to overhang the tops of the legs once assembled. For the crown (5), cut another square into four equal wedge-shaped pieces.

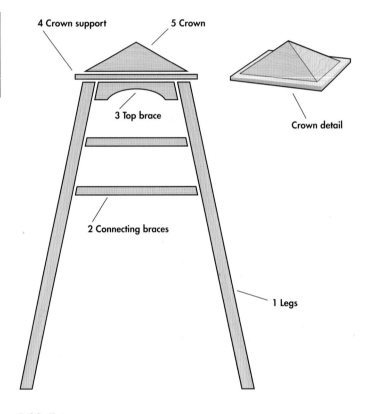

1-22 Tuteur.

These cuts will need to be at an angle, which will determine the pitch of the crown. For a crown with a 45-degree pitch, set the blade of the circular saw at a 45-degree angle, cut the wedges, and then fit them together using wood glue. Wood cement can be used to fill any gaps, and the entire structure can be painted.

CHAPTER 2

Structure for Dimension

A simple melody played on a pennywhistle can be very pretty. Add voice and you have a more dimensional composition. Now bring in a cello, perhaps some violins, a few flutes, and a kettle drum, and you have something far greater—you possibly have a symphony. You have dimensionality achieved through the interplay of a variety of elements creating a unified, harmonious composition **(2-1)**. Structure, or hardscape, can help attain dimensionality, in a variety of ways, both very simply and with considerable complexity. We will begin by looking at simple uses of structure to add dimensionality to a garden and then move on to more complex expressions of dimensionality.

2-1 At the simplest level, plants with architectural definition can themselves serve as structural elements through their definitive simplicity of form. Here Allium adds structural definition to a planting.

Simple Additions

Dimensionality can be very subtle. Yet the effect of providing some structural component to add just a hint of another dimension can be very satisfying, as this garden demonstrates.

In the digitally altered image shown in **2-2,** we see—well, not much—a few plants in a gravel field. A pennywhistle tune perhaps. In **2-3,** we see a structural element in the background, which definitely adds dimension to the scene. Another voice has been added. In the unaltered image **(2-4),** we see the garden as it is, with plants, groupings of stones, and wooden stakes forming an irregular fencelike structure. Perhaps not a symphony nor even a chamber music piece, but certainly a song in several voices with much more complexity and several levels of dimensionality—spatially, texturally, and in the quality of mass. This is what structural elements can bring to a garden.

The foreground stones give meaning to the Bergenia groupings through the relationships of contrast and harmony in form, texture, color, and mass. The broad leaves of *Bergenia cordifolia* contrast with the stones, as does the red bayberry (*Berberis atropurpureum,* 'Rose Glow'). In the middle ground is Phormium, picking up the red of the Bergenia and the Berberis. To the very rear, green bayberry echoes the form and leaf shape of the red bayberry while contrasting in color. These relationships of harmony and contrast add dimension to the garden.

The stones also relate to the gravel base, raising that medium upward. These stones repeat throughout the garden, adding strength and helping to unify the space. The wooden stakes, while adding textural contrast, raise the garden vertically, lifting it further off the horizontal plane.

A FEW THOUGHTS ON
Garden Relationships

Relationships are really what a garden is all about. When we combine plants, it is the way they relate to one another that determines how effective they are. Two harmonizing or contrasting plants give us more pleasure than one plant does alone. Similarly, an element can take on more meaning and purpose when in proximity to some other element with which it forms a visual relationship. In the course of creating gardens, we are aware of this instinctively. We put a favorite object among a few plants, or we make a grouping of objects that when seen together create a more meaningful whole. In this example, the Bergenia takes on more value and purpose as it groups around a collection of stones.

2-2 A modified view of the image in 2-4 with all the structural elements removed.

2-3 A modified view of 2-4 with the stones removed.

2-4 The garden as it truly is. Compare this with the images in 2-2 and 2-3.

Scale/Proportion

The larger stones seen only in relation to the pebble bed are certainly of sufficient size. They are perhaps a bit too large for the Bergenia, but definitely appropriate for the Berberis. The wooden stakes should certainly be no taller. Personally, I would have enjoyed a few stones twice as large as those shown for a more complete transition from base to top, but this may be simply a matter of taste.

Style

All elements in this garden work well together, all being of natural materials and of a somewhat waterfront feel with an informal Asian touch.

Additional Hardscape Functions

The stone groupings create *focal* areas, and the design of the post arrangements adds a degree of *ornamentation*.

Application

Under consideration here is not the particular garden, but the use of hardscape elements within the garden to add dimension. Simple components such as the rounded stones and the wooden stakes would be appropriate in a simple, sparsely planted garden where the intent was to convey a sense of natural space punctuated with pockets of plantings. In another type of garden—say, a mountain garden or a garden in the woods—where the aim was the same, outcroppings and tree stumps could be used to similar effect.

Planting

Berberis atropurpureum 'Rose glow,' *Bergenia cordifolia*, Phormium.

Suburban Terraces

Although suburban landscapes are often made up of a lawn with an abundance of foundation plantings at various elevations, they generally present themselves as two-dimensional. The plants around the house are often clipped into a continuous, nondescript mass and seem more a part of the home than the garden. The lawn is just there and so ubiquitously that we cease to see it as anything other than a flat sea of green around the house. The overall effect is one wanting in character and dimensionality.

This garden is a creation of mine, and I also used it in two of my other books for the following reason: I continue to come across too few gardens in suburban neighborhoods that demonstrate the concept of dimensionality. Though this example may not be spectacular, it is certainly different from what we usually find in suburbia the world over and it does demonstrate the effectiveness of dimensionality.

Initially, this garden was somewhat substandard for its type, only in that it didn't possess the quantity of foundation plantings that most yards have (2-5). Otherwise, it belonged to that paradigm that characterizes suburban America— a lawn with clipped shrubs clinging to the sides of the houses. Look down the lane in 2-6.

2-5 A fairly typical suburban front yard, but without the usual quota of foundation plants.

2-6 Uniformity characterizes many suburban neighborhoods.

2-7 The same yard in which walls were used to create several elevations, permitting a rich plethora of plantings.

In **2-7**, we find a fairly startling alteration, owing primarily to the inclusion of dimensional structures. Two walls were built, creating three elevations, which lift the eye from the lawn upward in a gradual ascent **(2-8)**. This rise through several dimensions helps to unite the home with the garden by bringing the garden more into scale with the home. The walls create strength, balance, and dimensionality and allow for a more diverse planting palette on several levels **(2-9** and **2-10)**.

Scale/Proportion

The walls are neither too many, too tall, nor too low **(2-8)**. This is true simply because each is half the vertical distance from the ground plane to the porch—mathematically, a natural choice. One of the purposes of the walls was to completely mask the concrete porch. One wall would have done that, but then it would have been too tall in relation to the ground plane. Two walls create a gradual transition. They do not cause the garden to dominate the house, nor do they shrink in relation to it. The planting is overabundant, for the purpose of immediate gratification and because that was the owner's wish.

2-8 The fabricated block walls bring dimensionality and strength to the yard, permitting several levels of planting.

2-9 The addition of elevated growing spaces allows for a lush planting scheme.

2-10 As in 2-9, elevated growing spaces allow for a lush planting scheme.

2-11 In this design, the yard doesn't break ranks with the neighborhood, in that the lawn remains; however, it is no longer a mere rectangle.

Style

The line that the walls were given releases the lawn from the typical rectangular conformation and, without breaking entirely from the surrounding environment of the neighborhood, presents a more graceful sweep of green between the plantings (2-11). A fabricated material, rather than natural stone, was used in the wall construction, which helps harmonize the garden with its surrounding world. There is clearly a sort of free-form style to the garden, though it is still somewhat controlled.

Additional Hardscape Functions

This garden and other gardens in this chapter could just as well have been discussed in Chapter 1 (Structure & Balance), because by providing dimension a garden does come more into balance with the home. However, dimensionality is a quality of its own that has a relation within the garden itself.

Application

If you think of the millions of suburban yards, front and back, the possibilities for adding dimensionality are enormous. Generally, dimensionality is a quality necessary for all gardens, in some appropriate scale and style, but particularly if the spaces are fairly featureless and flat.

Planting

The tall grass, maiden grass (*Miscanthus sinensis 'Gracillimus'*), provides a striking accent and obscures the porch. Also in prominence are Rugosa rose (*Rosa rugosa*), bigleaf hydrangea (*Hydrangea macrophylla*), Japanese umbrella pine (*Sciadopitys verticillata*), false cypress (*Chamaecyparis pisifera filifera 'Aurea Nana'*), a variety of Iris, daylilies, Azaleas (*Rhododendron* x), and other shrubs and perennials.

Stylized Design in Stone

Retaining walls can be wonderful hardscape elements. They provide additional planting areas, making use of the vertical spaces. As we saw in the last garden, they also contribute strength, giving the garden greater permanence, and they bring character and dimensionality to the setting.

In the "before" shot **(2-12),** we see a completely undeveloped garden waiting to be discovered. All too often, such a space would have been planted and a patio perhaps added—this would have been attractive and usable, but it would have lacked dimensionality.

The rear of the property was a little higher than the rest, and it was that slightly raised area at the rear that brought to mind the notion of creating raised beds **(2-13).** Raised beds would give the garden strength and dimensionality, helping to create a balance against the surrounding buildings.

One continuous wall at the same elevation would have achieved this. However, creating different elevations, with the grass bench and the built-in stone tables, achieves a greater depth of structural dimensionality. In addition, by somewhat emulating the surroundings on a smaller scale, they help to bring about unity.

2-12 As there was no specific need to create different elevations, this site would typically have been left as one plane.

2-13 The raised beds bring dimensionality, definition, and strength to the garden.

2-14 Various levels add to the dimensionality.

As with our pennywhistle tune, another layer of complexity has been added. Also, bringing the wall inward into the garden begins to create horizontal dimensionality, explored further in our next examples **(2-14)**.

Scale/Proportion
The walls are about as tall as they could be without overpowering the living space, and the grass bench and the stone tables next to the benches help anchor the walls in the garden. The beds that the walls form are approximately 2 feet deep, which is adequate for planting without encroaching too much on the available space **(2-15)**.

Style
Natural materials predominate in an intentionally stylized fashion. Water issues from the wall **(2-16)**, flowing into the water garden, from which it is recirculated back through the wall. Being of a different medium, the water garden also

2-15 It is important that raised beds such as these be neither too small, thus seeming insignificant, nor too large, as to dominate the space.

2-16 Water recirculates through the wall.

2-17 Stone tables were built in to ensconce the tiled benches.

2-18 The benches add ornamentation to the garden.

helps in providing another level of dimensionality. It also contributes to the overall "arts-and-crafts" style, characterized by the skillful working of natural materials into a unified composition.

Additional Hardscape Functions

The benches are nestled between stone tables (designed for this purpose), and they add a pleasant touch of *ornamentation* **(2-17** and **2-18)**. This garden could have been used to exemplify using structure for *outdoor living* as well.

Application

A property need not be sloped to comfortably accommodate raised beds. Many flat spaces in urban, suburban, village, and rural settings would benefit from this sort of dimensionality. Along with adding a vertical accent, such walls provide strength and durability, helping to create a permanent space in which the plants can be varied while the overall garden endures. Where there are pets or children, raised beds can provide protected planting spaces. Raised beds also give instant height to the planting and can help create privacy.

Planting

Japanese Stewartia (*Stewartia pseudocamellia*), Leland cypress (*Cupressocyparis leylandii*), and Japanese cedar (*Cryptomeria japonica*) lend vertical accents to the planting beds. There are many shrubs, including *Hydrangea paniculata, Kerria japonica, Hydrangea macrophylla,* and, for its bright variegations, tatarian dogwood (*Cornus alba 'Argenteo-marginata'*). Around the pool are Andromeda (*Pieris* x), Spirea (*Spirea* x *vanhouttei*), Daphne (*Daphne odora*), and threadleaf maple (*Acer palmatum dissectum*).

Horizontal Dimension

As mentioned in the previous example, it is very easy for urban gardens to seem overwhelmed by their surroundings unless they are given some internal strength. This is especially true if they are very small and the surrounding structures quite large. In such cases, it is not only the addition of the hardscape but using the hardscape to create a well-defined space that creates the feeling of security.

As with the last garden, this next space was also deprived, as it lacked any structure or any sort of garden **(2-19)**. Raised beds were not needed specifically. Dimension, however, was. This finished garden could just as well have been used in Chapter 4 (Structure for Delineating Space), though it has a particularly apt lesson to convey here **(2-20)**. The bottleneck of the brick wall does indeed create a separate garden room, but it does more. Along with creating vertical dimension, stepping the wall inward toward the center of the garden creates horizontal dimensionality **(2-21)**. It is not just living space surrounded by garden, but living space that gives way to garden that gives way to living space. There is a rhythmic dynamic generated by these horizontal fluctuations **(2-22** and **2-23)**.

A FEW THOUGHTS ON
Scale in Small Spaces

In small gardens, it is important to scale down if you wish to increase the sense of space. Walls that would normally be 18 inches tall become 16- or 14-inch walls. Planting beds shrink as much as possible, while permitting sufficient planting. Furniture should likewise be scaled down, and pots and other ornaments kept on the smaller side. With everything scaled down and in proportion to everything else, the space will feel considerably larger.

Scale/Proportion

As this is a very small space, approximately 14 feet wide and 35 feet deep, the walls were kept low so as not to dominate the space, but made tall enough to serve their purpose of adding dimension and strength. The depth of the beds is similarly small—in some places only about 6 inches, at the bottleneck several feet—but large enough to plant abundantly overall.

Style

The style here is sort of a blend of arts and crafts, natural, and contemporary themes, utilizing Tennessee Crab Orchard stone for the paving, brick for the

2-19 A narrow, urban site can seem overwhelmed by surrounding buildings.

2-20 Given strength and purpose, the garden now stands up to the surrounding world, while providing a private haven within it.

retaining walls, and cedar for the lattice. There is a slight Asian touch to the design inspired by the owner.

Additional Hardscape Functions

As mentioned, this is a good example of using structure to *define spaces*. The water garden at the rear is a *focal point* **(2-22).** The curve and the narrowing of the walls create a sense of *motion* and provide *privacy* as well.

Application

This technique of building from the outside in could be used for most any garden to bring greater dimensionality. In a larger garden, creating different vertical

2-21 Paving of Tennessee Crab Orchard stone adds warmth.

2-22 Outdoor dining is now an option.

2-23 Lush planting softens the structural elements.

elevations (tiering) as well as horizontal variations would also be quite effective. If your space is pleasant but seems flat and uninteresting, try adding elements from high to low, outside to inside.

Planting

Purple sand cherry (*Prunus* x *cistena*) and weeping cherry (*Prunus subhirtella 'Pendula'*) provide vertical accents and privacy, as do crepe myrtle (*Lagerstroemia*) and Japanese cedar (*Cryptomeria japonica*). Many vines, grasses, and groundcovers contribute to the setting.

Sculpture Plinth
on a Terraced Platform

Often gardens are designed as planting beds around an open interior. When we bring the garden inward, toward the interior, we create another horizontal dimension by infusing the plane of the interior with the taller plane of the garden.

Here, in **2-24**, we have an elegant expression of structure used to add dimension, and as with the last garden, it does so both vertically as well as horizontally, bringing drama to the setting. Without this sculpted creation and the stone-edged steps, this would be a pretty scene but without much impact. The structural element raises the garden from the ordinary to the exceptional and gives it a depth otherwise lacking.

Although very different in style from the structural components in the last three gardens, this structure has a similar effect. By means of this sculpted creation, the garden rises from the base level through several levels of elevation. It then culminates in the monolith, which takes the eye to the upper level, defined by the top of the fence. On the horizontal plane, it pushes away from the strictly defined border of the garden, out into the garden, and provides palpable relief from the flat planes of the fence and base. The planter behind the sculpture begins this escape from two-dimensionality that finds completion in the sculpture and the platforms upon which it rests. Without this, the garden would have looked very restricted and felt very restricting.

Scale/Proportion

Scale here has been well considered. Every plane of perception is occupied with elements of interest such that there is a clear ascent from the lawn level to the top of the fence and beyond, with no plane dominating any other. At least from this corner of the garden, there is a gradual and graceful ascent from bottom to top, and from outside to inside, largely because of this sculpture and the planter behind it.

Style

The style is clearly contemporary and highly controlled, with a strong architectural component. Nothing is left to "do its own thing." If there were any portion of this garden that might seem arbitrary, it would be the fairly eclectic planting in the raised planter behind the monolith.

Additional Hardscape Functions

This garden could have been used to exemplify structure for *focal* interest, and it is certainly *ornamental* as well. The lessons it teaches in adding dimension, however, appropriately place it here.

Application

If we focus our attention on the function that this creation serves and how it serves it, rather than on its style, we can easily imagine countless applications. If you have a plain planted patio and want to add vertical and horizontal dimensions, place some arrangement of objects in one corner or the center. Even a grouping of planted pots could have this same effect if well arranged. On a large, open space such as a lawn, define an area with, say, a half circle of plants and put some solid object within the planting—you will see how the dimensionality of the space expands.

Planting

Birches (*Betula nigra*) provide the vertical accent. Behind the sculpture are *Acer palmatum* with its red leaves, Viburnum with its white blooms, and coverings of juniper, Mugo pine (*Pinus mugo*), and brightly flowering Astilbe.

2-24 Vertical and horizontal dimensionality created through the sculpture and platform.

Multiple Dimensions

Many gardeners, but particularly those who focus primarily on plants rather than space, often neglect the vertical potential of a given garden area. Here, we have a garden in which every dimensional possibility has been utilized for maximum effect **(2-25).**

This inviting tiered garden is a wonderful example of how beautifully multiple dimensions can be developed in a garden. From side to side and front to back, the garden offers an array of vistas through a continuum of elevations from ground to sky. We can see there is a world beyond, but that other world ceases to exist for us as this one claims all of our attention.

Of course, the magnificent planting arrangement contributes to the effectiveness of this garden, but without the structural components, we would be lost in a jungle of leaves and flowers. The stone structures serve to balance with the planting as well as articulate definite planes of dimensionality, creating a rich and complete composition.

Scale/Proportion

I enjoy the sense of proportion demonstrated here. The fountain could have been slightly lower without ill effect, but it works well as it is. It also could have been a bit smaller without making the rear retaining walls and planters seem too dominant. This would have had the effect of throwing the surrounding planting beds into more prominence, but that probably was not the aim, and the overall result seems just fine.

Style

In layout, this is a classical, formal design that is well balanced and proportioned. However, the abundant plants, especially the flowering plants, give this setting more of an English garden feeling. Had there been more uniformity of species and fewer flowering plants, the formality would have been accentuated, but I think it would not have been so much fun.

2-25 Multiple dimensions radiate throughout this tiered garden.

Additional Hardscape Functions

Balance and *ornamentation* are clearly evident here. The fountain is a *focal point* and provides the element of *motion*.

Application

This sort of garden could be scaled to a considerably smaller or larger area, but there would need to be the possibility of adding a rear retaining wall, making a sloped site most suitable. It would make a fine city garden or could be part of an estate garden, but would probably look out of place in suburbia.

Planting

There are too many species here to list them all. Most prominent are several varieties of juniper, Japanese maples, grasses, *Euonymus* sp., ivies, Hostas, Rhododendron, and Iris.

Dimensionality
in an English Garden

Rarely, in my view, should sloped yards remain sloped. In rear yards their only use is for kids to roll or sleigh down, and in front yards they have no use, can be dangerous, and are tiresome. Sloped property, however, has much potential and, when terraced rather than ignored, can be transformed into a dynamic, exciting landscape **(2-26)**.

In the "before" shot, we see a sloped, expressionless expanse of lawn, its most salient feature being an utter lack of dimensionality. As a landscape designer, I am always pleased when presented with such a property because of the potential such slopes possess. How much more exciting and satisfying these spaces become when freed from their confinement to a single plane and their real attributes discovered and utilized.

As with the first garden presented in this chapter (pages 28 to 30), vertical dimensionality was achieved simply by building two curving walls, creating three elevations **(2-27)**. In this garden, however, the walk was woven through the walls, rather than placed at their ends. This enhances the experience of the several planes, in that we can actually walk through them. The winding path intensifies the sense of amplitude, as we weave through and interact with the garden, both visually and physically **(2-28)**.

Scale/Proportion

The scale of the walls, in elevation, was simply a result of dividing the vertical distance from ground to top of grade (approximately 5 feet) by two, resulting in

> ## A FEW THOUGHTS ON
> ### Praise for the Problem Site
> Often people think of sloped properties as liabilities—as problem sites. I appreciate such sites because of their rich and varied potential. True, it is generally more expensive to render such sites into really usable spaces, but the results can be so much more dramatic, offering varied experiences and visual delights. Streams, waterfalls, and pools, rock outcrops, walled terraces, and hidden grottoes are only a few of the possibilities inherent in a sloped site. This same principle applies to many sorts of "problem" sites. Generally, a problem is only a question seeking an answer, and dipping into the creative well to find that answer can be richly rewarding.

2-26 A featureless plot in need of dimensionality.

2-27 Terracing with stone walls created three level areas out of one plane, providing the bones for the garden.

2-28 Stone is an enduring, appealing material that combines well with plants. There are many kinds of stone from which to choose.

two walls approximately 30 inches high. From front to back, each of the planes created by the walls was made large enough so as not to cause the viewer to feel restricted, and no one space dominated another **(2-29)**.

Style

This was intended to be an informal English garden **(2-30)**. The walls are dry-laid, with tiles and bricks worked in here and there. The walk is on sand in a running-bond pattern, with the outer basket-weave courses laid in cement. Just as brick is incorporated into the wall, stone is placed intermittently in the walk, serving to unite the two structures, while adding a quality of informal charm. The planting is eclectic, abundant, and comprises trees, shrubs, perennials, and annuals, in the manner of the English cottage garden **(2-31)**.

Additional Hardscape Functions

This garden could have been used just as well to exemplify the use of structure to create *motion*, and in fact other images of this garden are found in Chapter 3 (Structure for Instilling Motion). The walls, in their graceful sweep, and the

2-29 The brick walk picks up the curve of the lower wall and winds up through the upper wall, suggesting the quality of motion.

2-30 The result, once the construction was completed and the planting done, is a multidimensional landscape that is enjoyable to see and through which to pass.

2-31 The height of each wall is simply the difference in elevation from bottom to top divided by two. Their placement gives ample space to each level so that no one space dominates or is dominated.

walk infuse the garden with this quality of motion, while permitting an abundance of planting by providing structural *balance*.

Application

The many sloped properties so often covered in lawn and left otherwise undeveloped would in most cases benefit from this sort of structuring. Even very steep grades can be turned into useful, beautiful gardens in this manner.

Planting

To the rear is a weeping cherry (*Prunus subhirtella* 'Pendula'), a *Rhododendron maximum,* and climbing roses. Mixed all about are hollyhocks *(Alcea rosea),* various Iris, poppy (*Papaver*), lavender (*Lavendula* sp.), Cosmos (*Cosmos bipinnatus*), speedwell (*Veronica* sp.), heaths (*Erica* sp.), and heathers (*Calluna* sp.).

Textured-Concrete-Block Wall

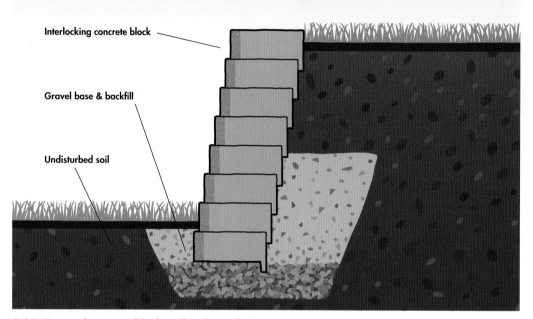

Interlocking concrete block

Gravel base & backfill

Undisturbed soil

2-32 Textured-concrete-block wall with interlocking concrete blocks, side view.

YOU WILL NEED
Concrete block, crushed stone and/or stone dust, level

There are a variety of products that will allow you to build a serviceable dry-laid retaining wall, with no particular skills. Some are so designed as to "lock" together, permitting a higher wall—to 4 feet or higher **(2-32).** Others are designed for walls no taller than 2 feet. Some look more like stone, some more like concrete, but all are more natural-looking than poured concrete.

No artistic skill is required in using most of these block types, and very little technical know-how is necessary to build a durable wall. The only demand on your physical abilities, apart from lifting the blocks and placing them, has to do with the creation of the bed in which the bottom course is to be laid **(2-33).** The only difficulty here is to ensure that the bed is level. If working with a variable grade, you can step the wall up or down as needed—just be sure that each course is level throughout its length.

Generally, a bed of at least 4 inches of compacted crushed rock is recommended as the final base for the bottom course. In temperate areas and where drainage is very good, this is not necessary, but it is still a good idea in part because a bed of crushed stone or stone dust is often easier to level than soil.

Once a level bed has been made, the rest is simply a matter of placing each block, course by course, until the desired height is reached. For the types of blocks that form a tight fit, it is also good to backfill behind the walls, once built, with about a foot of crushed stone to facilitate drainage and reduce water pressure.

This type of wall will always have a somewhat manufactured look—it can never be mistaken for a natural stone wall. But it looks attractive and there's much less expenditure in terms of time and money **(2-34).**

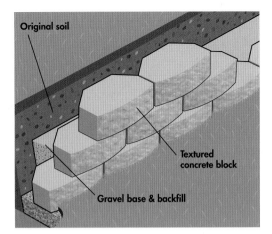

2-33 Textured-concrete-block wall with interlocking concrete blocks.

2-34 Concrete-block walls will always have a somewhat manufactured look.

Brick Walk with Mortared Outer Course

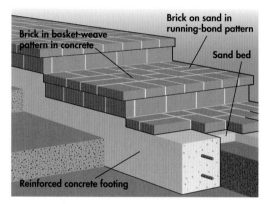

2-35 Brick walk with mortared outer course.

Even in temperate climates, it can be useful to build a brick walkway with the outer courses in concrete, to prevent the sand from washing out from under the inner courses of brick. In very temperate climates that do not experience freezing temperatures, the concrete does not need reinforcing with rebar. If freezing is likely, the rebar will allow the cement to move as a unit and will prevent it from cracking should frost heaving occur.

Excavate the path to a depth that will allow for a couple of inches of sand below the brick **(2-35).** Lay out the bricks across the area where the path is to go with the joints between the bricks and the path itself at the desired width. If no joint is desired, place the inner courses, edge to edge, but leave ½ inch between the bricks that are to be in concrete.

Brick can be laid in a variety of patterns. In this example, the inner courses of the brick are in a running-bond pattern, in which the end joints of two bricks touching within a linear course are spanned by the middle of the bricks on either side. The outer courses, in concrete, are in a basket-weave pattern, in which two bricks are laid in the same direction next to each other and the next two are laid perpendicularly to the first two.

Remove the outer courses of bricks, and begin setting the inner courses. Using a rubber mallet, firmly tap each brick into place. When

several bricks are down, place a 2-foot length of two-by-four across several courses of brick and check for level. With a stone hammer, firmly tap the two-by-four to set the bricks at the same level.

To place the outer courses, dig a trench for each. If necessary, build a wooden form to contain the concrete (see also Chapters 7 and 8). The depth will depend on the depth of frost, as the bottom of the concrete should be below the frost line. Place the bottom rebar several inches from the bottom of the trench with stones beneath every several feet to support it. Drive several vertical lengths of rebar into the soil every few feet, making sure the top of the rebar will be embedded in the concrete. Wire the top and bottom pieces of rebar to the vertical piece, and be certain both horizontal lengths of rebar are in the middle of the trench from side to side.

There is quite a variance in suggested mixes for concrete, but a middle-of-the-road approach would be a mix of approximately one part cement, two-and-one-half parts sand, and three parts small gravel. Mix with water, pour the thick slurry of concrete into the trench or form to

2-36 Joints between bricks can be filled by sweeping sand, soil, or a sand-cement mix into them.

approximately ½ inch above the bottom of the brick, and set the brick into place, level with the bricks already set on the sand. Use the 2-foot level to check this. Fill the joints between the bricks with the concrete mix. Alternatively, you can put concrete only in the outermost parts of the joints if you prefer to have a sand- or soil-fill look, as long as the bricks are well set within the concrete. The concrete on the outer portions of the joints will contain the sand or soil, which can then be host to moss or small plants.

If there are to be steps, the risers will need to be set in concrete or the bricks set firmly into the ground in "soldier" courses—that is, standing on end. Even then, they should be anchored firmly to prevent any movement. If a joint was left between the bricks set on the sand, the joints can be filled by sweeping sand, soil, or a sand-concrete mix into them, depending on the look desired **(2-36).**

Dry-Laid Stone Wall

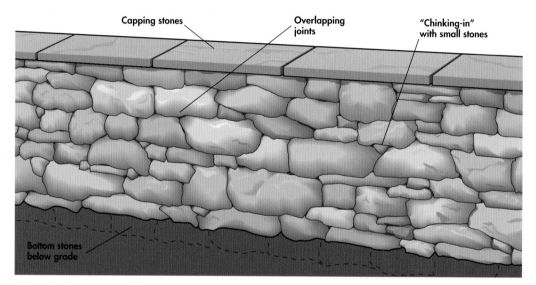

Capping stones

Overlapping joints

"Chinking-in" with small stones

Bottom stones below grade

2-37 Dry-laid stone wall.

YOU WILL NEED
Stones of various sizes, capping stones, crushed stone or gravel, rubble

The illustration in **2-37** shows the front of a wall built with stones in a variety of sizes, but all fairly rectangular. This is the easiest sort of stone with which to work. Odd shapes can make for an interesting wall but require more skill in using them **(2-38** and **2-39). **Three to five sizes of rectangular stone used in the same wall will create an ashlar pattern, which is especially effective when the various sizes are distributed evenly, but randomly **(2-40).**

To build a dry wall, you need to dig a trench, and if you are in an area that freezes, it needs to be filled with crushed stone or gravel to create a foundation that drains. Large stones go in the trench for the footing. Unless it is a very low wall, it is generally a good idea to build the wall with a very slight pitch into the hill it is retaining—this batter will counter the pressure of soil over time. It is also a good idea to have an occasional stone that extends back into the hill to function as a kind of anchor. The wall should be backfilled with rubble (broken or small pieces of stone) or some other stone material as the wall goes up, to fill in the gaps and ensure a solid construction.

2-38 Odd shapes can make for an interesting wall.

2-39 Odd shapes require more skill in using them.

2-40 Various sizes of rectangular stone are used in the same wall.

As illustrated in **2-41,** the joints are overlapped so that no vertical joint runs through more than three courses. (If you know of a wall that is falling down, whether in mortar or not, examine it. You will find that the cracks tend to appear along these long running joints.) There should be a fairly even distribution of sizes of stones, with larger stones lower down, smaller stones toward the top but still good-sized, and solid and flat stones forming the cap.

To create a planting pocket in the wall, simply leave a stone out, but span the space above the hole with a substantial stone supported firmly from below on both sides **(2-42** and **2-43).**

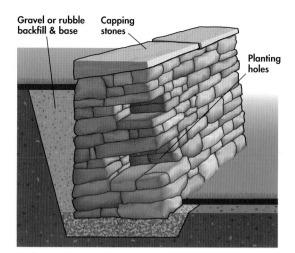

2-41 Drywall with holes.

2-42
Working on a drywall with holes.

2-43
Completed drywall with holes.

CHAPTER 3

Structure for Instilling Motion

One of the most wonderful attributes you can give a garden is the quality of motion. Without it, a garden is more static and considerably less engaging than it could be. No matter how small or how large the garden, a sensation of motion that invites us to explore it visually or to wander through it physically can be achieved.

Our choices of structures to create this desirable quality are essentially unlimited, although there are only four methods. One method is the creation of curving lines, as in a curved path, for example. There are situations, though, in which curved paths are not possible, so a second method is to produce the effect of a curve by jogging structural elements to either side of a centerline, creating a rhythmic flow. A third method is to have something actually in motion, such as moving water. The fourth method is creating a prominent element in the garden that embodies the quality of movement. In this chapter, we examine a variety of quite diverse gardens in which these methods were employed to achieve the graceful, inviting quality of motion.

Curving Suburbia

One of the simplest methods for creating a sense of motion is by establishing meandering sight lines we can follow visually or actual paths we can walk along. These need not be defined dramatically to be effective, as this garden in the suburbs of New York City shows.

In the "before" image **(3-1)**, we find the standard layout of the typical suburban garden, consisting of foundation planting, a lawn, and a specimen tree here or there. This formulaic approach has never been particularly successful as far as visual beauty and personal enjoyment are concerned, so why it has endured remains something of a mystery. I attribute it to imitation and a lack of better examples.

This landscape was a two-dimensional single-plane garden that was essentially monochromatic and totally static. The side yard was used primarily as a means of passage from front to back. Although it was highly visible from the house, the front and back yards, and the two streets, this space was completely uninteresting, unsatisfying, and uninviting.

The solution to these failings proved simple: The beds along the house were given more graceful form, and across from them, along the sidewalk, raised berm beds were created, also in a curving fashion. The mere addition of the berm beds on the sidewalk side had a huge impact on balancing the space with the house and creating a space with flowing motion through which we are invited to pass. The clearly defined path completes the sense of motion that this garden now conveys **(3-2).**

A curving walkway of tumbled bluestone, cut into the grass so that its surface is level with the lawn, defines this space as a stroll garden **(3-3).** The walk wraps from the front entry (which was also rebuilt and is the subject of the next project)

A FEW THOUGHTS ON
Building with Berms

One simple method of adding dimensionality to a flat garden site without bringing in boulders and such is to create berms. These mounds of soil can be made several feet tall, and their heights and widths varied for dramatic effect. They can be formed into most any shape and once planted will retain their character essentially forever with little maintenance. They provide instant and inexpensive dimension, allow for additional planting areas, and can dramatically transform a garden.

3-1 A fairly unattractive suburban yard lacking motion, balance, and dimensionality, due to the static planting along the house with nothing to balance against it.

3-2 Raised, curved berms on the right, curving beds on the left, and a curving walkway give a sense of motion.

3-3 The stones were laid out and the path walked before cutting them into the sod.

to the gate that leads into the backyard, following a meandering line that corresponds with the ins and outs of the plant beds (**3-4** and **3-5**).

These additional planting beds balance with the house through their dimensional mass, and they take on structural stature in relation to the lawn, which they contain and define much as would walls. They also relate with one another through a variety of harmonies and contrasts in line, density, form, size, texture, and color, and by doing this, add considerably to the sense of motion in the garden. An interplay takes place between the opposing plants and plant groupings that changes from day to day and month to month. There is no possibility for stasis in such a garden. Still, the density of plantings in these beds would benefit from some solid element, such as a large stone, placed amidst the abundant foliage (**3-6**).

3-4 A static corner of the property "before."

3-5 The same view as in 3-4 after the berms and the walk were created.

3-6 The view of the walk from the other end of the yard, presenting a rhythmic flow.

3-7 The curving walkway, seen in 3-2.

Scale/Proportion

There's really not much to say about scale here. The berms could have been larger perhaps but seem proportioned well enough as they are, and the path is a suitable width.

Style

Natural and lush with a free-form feel.

Additional Hardscape Functions

The outer beds help to *balance* the garden with the house, which otherwise would overpower the yard.

Application

The structural elements in this garden are mounds of soil that are shaped, placed, and planted so as to create gracefully flowing lines, and individual stones set into the curving swath of lawn delineated by the berms. Together, they create a rhythmic undulation in space and time through which we are invited to wander. Virtually every suburban yard made up of an expanse of lawn with foundation plants could benefit from this approach. Even without the stepping stones, the berms create sufficient structural definition to bring both balance and rhythmic motion to a static scene.

Planting

In the foreground (**3-7**) are smoke bush (*Cotinus coggygria*), Miscanthus, *Rosa rugosa*, and *Buddleia* sp. Further along are crepe myrtle (*Lagerstroemia* x), sand cherry (*Prunus* x *cistena*), Iris, Hemerocallis, Cytisus, Euonymus, and varieties of lavender. At the corner of the house is a Leland cypress, and nearby are Spirea, *Prunus x cistena*, Berberis, lamb's ears (Stachys), Dianthus, lavender, butterfly bush (Buddleia), and other shrubs and perennials.

Curving the Entry

I n the majority of homes, particularly in suburbia, entries and porches are (with some marvelous exceptions) entirely functional affairs conceived with the sole intent of getting us into the front door. A useful aim, certainly, with the design driven largely by budget concerns, but there must be other more exciting, pleasing, and graceful ways to approach the home than via a square concrete porch. Here, we look at one entry in which a sense of motion, so suitable to this area of the property, has been incorporated into the design **(3-8).**

This front entry belongs to the same house whose garden was discussed previously but utilizes a different technique to add the quality of motion. As the "before" images show, the original entry and entry porch looked fairly static and graceless **(3-9** and **3-10).** They were functional, but the blockish concrete porch and stiff, straight steps provided nothing in the way of pleasure or beauty for anyone coming or going.

Because the front door was often approached from the driveway on the left and from the sidewalk from either direction, the porch was given access from both sides. The curve of the front wall focuses the porch on the front door, while the two sets of flaring steps define the cross-axis. The bottom step is given greater depth in order to receive passage from the side or the front. In the rear, two planters visually anchor the porch to the home and permit a softening effect from the plants.

The sensation of motion is derived from several design elements working together **(3-11).** At the bottom are the staggered, tumbled bluestone steps that lead in an indirect line to the primary steps. These arc upward, angling in toward the house in a graceful sweep. The front supporting wall of the porch is curved rather than angular, and the railing forms a wavy line following the curve of the steps. The low wall in front reiterates the curve of the porch, accenting the dominant flowing line. The result is an entry with considerable style, providing a pleasant sense of movement along a gracefully curving line.

3-8 The new entry of Georgia Peach marble with curving steps.

3-9 "Before," a fairly typical entry porch—monolithic and static.

3-10 "Before," with the shrubs removed.

3-11 The porch now leads to the walk around the side of the house and to the sidewalk, on both sides.

Scale/Proportion

In considering scale, some fault may be found here. This is an imposing entry porch, both in terms of mass and design. It could be argued that the porch is overstated for this home, especially when seen in relation only to the lower story. However, when seen as a part of the entire two-story structure, the porch seems suitably scaled, though perhaps too dramatically designed for the house's fairly simple style of architecture. (In fact, though I designed and built this porch and do like the way it "moves," I feel that it is overmuch for this house.)

Style

This is an "arts-and-crafts" structure, built of Georgia Peach marble, with a brass railing.

Additional Hardscape Functions

There is certainly an *ornamental* quality to this entry, it adds another *dimension,* and it helps *balance* the home with the property.

Application

Such an entry would be best suited to an "artsy" style of a home of at least two stories or to a home of considerable mass in need of a prominent entrance.

Planting

Around the porch are oakleaf hydrangea, ferns, *Skimmia japonica,* Iris, Heucherella, and *Cornus alba.* The other beds generally have the same plants as the previous project (page 64), which is the same home and garden.

Along a Garden Path

Many homeowners seem to think that a large lawn in and of itself is the ultimate outdoor possession, and so miss developing the many possibilities inherent in their properties. They water the grass, they weed and fertilize, and they pay taxes on their properties, without getting much use out of them. As this project and others demonstrate, a great deal of enjoyment can be derived from doing more with the usual lawn area.

I was introduced to this garden through a friend and was quite taken with it **(3-12)**. I use different portions of it in several chapters, as the owner has utilized hardscape to such good effect (yet notice how luxuriant it is). Here, we look at what the garden teaches us in terms of instilling motion.

The narrow brick path winds through the garden, defining gracious planting beds on either side. As it meanders along its circuitous course to the rear and out the back gate, it takes us into different structured areas of the garden, affording charming views along the way.

As we move down the path **(3-13)**, it rounds a bend and straightens **(3-14 and 3-15)**. There, the water garden serves to eliminate stasis, with its tumbled stone, waterfalls, and swimming fish maintaining a sense of graceful flow and easy tempo **(3-16 and 3-17)**. Across from the water garden is a table and bench, and beyond, views into other portions of the garden, reached only by following the curving path **(3-18)**.

Moving along, we come to a garden house with a quiet place to sit and enjoy the scenery **(3-19)**. From here, we can wander toward the rear **(3-20)** or go explore other areas of the garden **(3-21)**. The effect of the winding brick path, the lush beds it defines, and the many garden areas to which it leads is simply delightful. It is a fun, inviting path to walk down or simply just to see, and the variety of experiences and sights it affords are completely charming and satisfying.

3-12 A brick walk weaves through the property.

3-13 The walk brings us to many garden scenes.

3-14 The walk leads to seating areas and past a fish pond.

3-15 Looking back toward the garden entry.

3-16 Where the path straightens, the waterfall takes over the job of providing motion.

3-17
The waterfall.

3-18 From places along the walk, views into other areas open up.

3-19 The walk leads from the rear entrance to a seating area beneath an arbor.

3-20 From the seating area, the curving walk winds out to the rear entrance.

3-21 Here, the walk opens up into a free-form patio edged in graceful perennial borders.

A FEW THOUGHTS ON

Amplifying by Repeating Forms

Notice the lovely harmony created among the curving swath of lawn, the iron arbor in the background, and the arching junipers behind that **(3-22)**. The three work together, repeating the same form and thereby amplifying the effect of each.

3-22 The sweeping swath of lawn, the arch of the arbor, and the two junipers leaning together amplify the harmony.

Scale/Proportion
Meant to be walked in single file, this narrow path has sort of a fairytale feel as it appears and disappears around bends. A wider path would have eliminated some of that charm.

Style
The style is completely free-form and informal around the path; however, there are more formal elements in this garden, discussed in the next chapter.

Additional Hardscape Functions
Here, we find structures for *defining space*, structures for creating *privacy*, and areas for *outdoor living*, as well as elements of *ornamentation* (see Chapters 4, 6, 7, and 8, respectively).

Application
This garden could serve as a model for any area large enough to contain a meandering path leading to a variety of garden spaces. Coming to mind are the many rural and suburban back and side yards that could benefit so much from such a design.

Planting
Along the upper path and around the lawn: Hemerocallis, Hosta, Dianthus, Dicentra, *Centaurea hypoleuca*, Cimicifuga, Artemisia

Midway down the path: Daylily, *Astilbe* sp., *Hosta* sp., Cimicifuga, Clematis, Phlox, lilies

Around the brick patio: Pink Geraniums, Impatiens, yarrow, lilies, Centaurea, Begonias, Monarda, Shasta daisy, *Lupinus* x 'Russell Hybrid,' Delphinium

A Pleasurable Passage

Many properties possess narrow spaces, which can be among the most difficult areas with which to work. When they must serve as a passageway, the walkway is usually made straight and planted only on one side. As this project shows, there are greater possibilities for such spaces and even in an area only 7 feet wide the quality of motion can be created.

The "before" image (3-23) of this side yard of a music conservatory was taken just after the concrete that extended from the iron fence to the building was removed and the below-grade building structure was waterproofed. Although there is only about 7 feet between the fence and the building, I wanted this walk area from the front along the side to the rear of the garden to be in keeping with the primary garden area. It needed to be graceful and possess the quality of movement seen in the primary garden (3-24).

The technique used here was to stagger the paving so that it alternately runs closer to the building and then staggers over to run close to the fence. The planting is continuous along both sides, but where the walkway jogs away from either the fence or the building, the planting is heavier on that side. This jogging of the walkway and alternate massing of plants along either side creates a sense of motion that is accentuated by using distinctive plants alternately on either side along the length of the walk (3-25). Particularly notable in this respect are the Leland cypress (*Cupessocyparis leylandii*) and the ornamental grasses (*Miscanthus sinensis 'Gracilimus'*).

Even though the space was very narrow and completely rectilinear, the sense of a curving line was achieved (3-26 and 3-27). Clearly, the primary purpose of this hardscape is to make passage possible from the front to the rear. The original concrete slab did this, but it provided no quality of motion nor afforded any other aesthetic satisfaction. Creating a bluestone walkway through a richly textured garden not only makes passage possible but provides a sense of graceful motion as well (3-28, 3-29, and 3-30).

3-23 Previously, this area had been covered by a slab of concrete.

3-24 The walkway jogs to either side, creating the sensation of movement.

3-25 Dramatic plants juxtaposed along both sides of the walk lead the eye onward.

3-26 The same view as in 3-27 before creating the walk and the planting beds.

3-27 The "after" view of 3-26.

Scale/Proportion

Although the space was very narrow, the walkway is ample and the planting abundant. Together, the walk and the planting balance well with the building, while the dimensions of the walk are in scale with the abundant plants.

Style

Although informal in nature and planted eclectically, this setting has a feeling of regularity, due to the quality of the stone, the perfect flatness of the walk, and the four 6-inch-rise steps.

3-28 Looking back to the front of the garden before building the new walk.

3-29 The "after" view of 3-28.

A FEW THOUGHTS ON
Curving Rectangles

It is very easy to create curving paths using rectangular stones. Simply draw out the curve on whatever material the path is going on, and place the paving stones so that they balance along that line by extending outward more or less equally, but not identically, to either side. Then plant the borders between the stones with groundcover that will mask the edges, and the result will be a curved path.

3-30 A gracious space adorned by graceful plants.

Additional Hardscape Functions
Dimensionality and *balance.*

Application
There are many narrow sites—along the sides of homes, between buildings, or along path lines from driveways to the front doors, for example—that could benefit from this approach.

Planting
Lagerstroemia arch over the walk. *Cupressocyparis lelandii* form vertical accents, while numerous shrubs and perennials—including Spirea, oakleaf hydrangea, Euonymus, sand cherry, Pieris, Yucca, daylily, Iris, *Hydrangea petiolaris*, Miscanthus, Berberis, and Cytisus—make up the remainder.

An Elegant *S*

The shortest distance between two points is indeed a straight line, but rarely is a straight line the most appealing. Adding just a little curve to a walkway can have a remarkably agreeable effect, which can be enhanced by dramatic planting.

A technique similar to the one employed in the last garden is used here. This was the natural location for the primary approach to the front of the home from the circular drive **(3-31)**. It was sloped, however, and a sloping walkway is neither appealing nor safe where winters are severe, which was the case here. Consequently, the slope needed to be terraced while creating a comfortable and attractive walkway. The solution can be seen in **3-32.**

3-31 The natural location for the walk to the front of the house—looking up from the drive.

3-32 A bluestone walk edged in Belgium block curves up through graceful plantings.

In walking up this path, we now follow a graceful, shallow *S* curve, delineated by the individual platforms of bluestone edged in Belgium block and punctuated here and there with large boulders. Because there is a straight line of sight up and down the path, the curve is more experiential than visual, carrying us through a wide sweep about midway. Also contributing to the graceful sense of motion is the gentle upward lift, easily navigated through the series of 5-inch rises from level to level. And, as in the last garden (pages 75 to 79), distinctive plants are alternately placed along both sides, drawing the eye through the length of the walkway.

This design approach not only creates a safe and comfortable passage, but it also provides an element of mild excitement through its gradual ascent and descent and the appearance at odd niches of large boulders **(3-33 and 3-34).**

3-33 Looking down from the patio before the walk was installed.

3-34 Looking down from the patio after completion.

3-35 Dramatic plants staggered along the walk accentuate the sense of movement.

3-36 Grasses, Cornus, Caryopteris, juniper, and Potentilla comprise the primary plant groupings.

Scale/Proportion

The path is quite broad, filling the available space quite well, yet it does not overpower the house nor is it overpowered by it, and it is balanced by the amplitude of planting. This is a long walkway, but it would have seemed even longer and more insubstantial had it been made narrower.

Style

"Rural elegant" might characterize this style, as the design is clearly not classical nor is it naturalistic. But such a broad sweep of stairs always conveys a quality of refined gracefulness.

Additional Hardscape Functions

As the "before" images demonstrate, a slope without some form of terracing is rather featureless and two-dimensional. Clearly, the steps bring *dimensionality* to the space.

Application

Such stairs are suitable only for a fairly large, slightly sloped expanse leading to a fairly elegant structure. They would look completely out of place in a cramped setting and pretentious in a less dignified one.

Planting

Grasses, Caryopteris, junipers, Potentilla, and *Cornus alba* are the primary plants here (**3-35** and **3-36**).

A Romantic Tangle

Another way to instill the quality of motion into a garden is to create something that actually moves, such as a stream **(3-37** and **3-38)**. But can a stream be considered a hardscape component? As you might surmise, my answer is a resounding "Yes!" Once you have constructed one, you'll agree.

This particular stream required approximately $3^{1}/_{2}$ tons of stone to create the infrastructure—quite a considerable quantity of hardscape **(3-39** and **3-40)**. Although grown over with a remarkable plethora of species, the stones have kept their structural value. Placed so as to create gracefully "moving" lines and filled with flowing, splashing, gurgling water, this animated waterworks brings a dazzling dimension to the garden. You really have to be here to appreciate how captivating this garden is.

3-37 Before construction—a forlorn plot of ground.

3-38 The same view as in 3-37 after creating a stream garden.

3-39 Seven-thousand pounds of stone were used in building the stream.

3-40 One stone can weigh as much as 1,500 pounds.

3-41 The water is recirculated from the koi pond to the artesian well.

3-42 West wall of the sculpture court.

3-43 Although the stream is intended to be enjoyed mainly from the sculpture court, there are two seating areas beneath weeping cherry trees.

3-44
Flowing
water vivifies
the garden.

3-45 Plants thrive and naturalize near the constant moisture.

3-46 The fish swim upstream, leaping the cascades.

The stream begins at the far end of the garden as an artesian well, spilling about two thousand gallons of water an hour over a waterfall into a shallow basin, from which it flows on down through the garden to the koi pond. From there, it recirculates below ground back to the source **(3-41)**. Although it is meant to be enjoyed primarily from the adjoining sculpture court **(3-42)**, there are two seating areas within the garden, both tucked beneath weeping cherry trees **(3-43)**. Difficult to appreciate from mere images, this ever-flowing body of water, as it laps the sides of the stones, gives life to the garden to an astonishing degree **(3-44, 3-45,** and **3-46)**.

Scale/Proportion

The stream runs the length of the garden from the far right corner to the near left, but occupies only a few feet of width, leaving plenty of planting space. It is neither dominated by nor dominates the surrounding garden. It could have been a little wider, with a slightly greater flow of water, but if smaller, would lose its impact. A significantly greater quantity of water running through the garden would probably have destroyed the Arcadian quality of the scene.

Style

Completely naturalistic.

Additional Hardscape Functions

Dimensionality and *outdoor living* from the sculpture court.

Sometimes it's best not to know what we are getting into. I ordered these stones by size and had them delivered, not realizing their density and weight. I found I could not get good placement by trying to handle them without the assistance of some kind of lifting device. After going through several industrial equipment and tool sources and three ironworks shops, I finally found a shipbuilder who manufactured this machine for me **(3-47)**. It comes apart into four pieces and can be carried by two men through a brownstone. The horizontal beam pivots about 160 degrees. A trolley runs the length of the horizontal beam, to which a hoist is attached. Using it, we were able to get precise placement of the stones.

3-47 The "Machine."

Application

This is a small, urban backyard, so if a stream works here, it could work just about anywhere, other than a suburban front yard.

Planting

Here we find Aralia, red-twigged dogwood and flowering dogwood, climbing red rose, weeping cherry (*Prunus subhirtilla* 'Snowcloud'), Japanese Anemone, Dicentra, Iris, Daphne, Wisteria, sweet woodruff, Viburnum, and lilac. There are oakleaf hydrangea (*Hydrangea quercifolia*), Hosta, fragrant Azalea, Pennisetum, Columbine, and Clematis. We also see boxwood, Cryptomeria, Leland cypress, Ilex, *Hydrangea macrophylla*, ferns and bracken, tufts of Campanula, and violets, as well as pansies.

Curvaceous Patio with Rill

Often patios and other structural elements designed for outdoor living are fairly static forms that are usually rectangular. Regardless of the materials employed, such structures can be made to embody the quality of motion, as we have seen already. It is all a question of design.

Flowing as a river from the arched steps off the upper terrace to the cascading steps below, this patio offers a variety experiences and views **(3-48)**. The upper terrace off the back porch is a great place to enjoy a morning cup of coffee or an evening glass of wine, while taking in the pleasing views around the patio and the panorama below **(3-49** and **3-50).**

3-48 Patio, walls, water garden, and steps combine to create a space in motion.

3-49 The upper terrace affords a view of the landscape below.

3-50 The terrace steps flow out toward the pool, which curves into the patio.

3-51 The splash pool/hot tub spills into a rill.

3-52 The rill flows along the patio and splashes down into a basin below.

3-53 The curved forms of the hardscape delineate graceful spaces.

3-54 The lower steps lead to a terrace overlooking the landscape below.

From this terrace, steps spill out into the patio, juxtaposed with the water feature across from it **(3-51)**. The wall along the greenhouse sweeps around to embrace the water feature, which spills into a channel winding along the patio edge and splashes into a lower basin **(3-52)**. From here, we can descend to another landing overlooking the landscape below. The combination of all these structural elements creates a graceful, flowing motion through wonderfully delineated spaces **(3-53** and **3-54)**.

Scale/Proportion

There is a nice balance between the various areas and elements, although perhaps a greater hardscape-to-plants ratio exists than would suit most tastes. Just about any component of this landscape could have been larger or smaller, depending on the desired effect, but as it is, it seems to work quite well.

Style
All the hardscaping—the patio, the walls, the pool, and the steps—is of textured concrete, so in this respect, the style is contemporary. However, the forms are all organic in design with relaxed lines, giving the garden as a whole a more natural feeling.

Additional Hardscape Functions
Structure here is used very well to *delineate space,* but because so much motion was created in these forms, it is appropriately placed in this chapter. Also evident are the wonderful opportunities for *outdoor living.*

Application
Here, the same sorts of elements found in many gardens have been given curving forms and placed in relationship to one another so as to generate a feeling of motion. This basic approach could be applied anywhere that these kinds of components—patio, walls, water features, stairs, and so on—are employed.

Planting
Dahlias, calla lilies, fig, Yucca, *Lobelia tupa, Phormium tenax* 'Lemon Wave,' Banksia, *Salvia guaranitica,* and others.

Frozen Motion

The quality of motion can be embodied or embedded within a structure. On the one hand, such a structure is the least effective method for conveying the liberating sense of movement. On the other, once perceived, such a structure can be the most effective type in eliciting our attention and heightening our appreciation. The following project is a case in point **(3-55)**.

   This is a fairly simple garden that is designed to provide young children with a playing area and adults with a place to sit and enjoy the outdoors **(3-56)**. A slight sense of motion is derived from the juxtaposed masses of plants, though the primary element of motion is found in the wall and the patio **(3-57)**.

3-55 The garden "before."

3-56 A garden for children and adults.

3-57 The patio was built to impart flowing motion, using the lines of the joints and the grain of the stone in the wall.

The patio has a free-form design. It is laid out in irregular shapes of bluestone and in a pattern in which all the lines move from the outer edge toward the center, generating a sense of movement toward a destination.

Similarly, the wall was built such that the grain of the stones creates sweeping lines from the bottom right and the bottom left, converging in the center. Normally, such walls are built with respect to the shapes of the stones only, as with a puzzle in which all the lines of the grain and the joints are canceled by contradictory lines. If a stone fits a space, it is placed there, with no respect to its other qualities. Here, care was taken to recognize and utilize the locked-in "frozen" energy of the stones, as seen in their grain and shape, to create a structure with vitality and movement. See **3-57** and Project 3C, "Veneer Wall," which follows on page 102.

Scale/Proportion

The wall in relation to the entire yard is of a suitable scale, and the patio and wall are a good balance. The patio itself could have been larger and seems too small in relation to the grass and the planted area; however, not shown is another patio at the near end that rectifies this seeming imbalance.

Style

This wall of Velvet Gray stone and the bluestone patio have sort of an "arts-and-crafts" style.

3-58 *Prunus cistina, Cotinus coggygria,* Berberis, and *Rosa rubrifolio* contrast nicely with the yellow tagate, the red Hemerocallis, and the white Clematis.

Additional Hardscape Functions

Outdoor living is certainly one of the purposes for the patio and little water garden, and the wall possesses a definite *ornamental* quality.

Application

All too often stone structures are built with no regard for the particular qualities of the individual stones. Some types of stones evince no distinguishing characteristics one from another, and not much can be done with them apart from building sound structures. Stones that do have grain and color variations, however, can be employed to create all manner of structures that embody a sense of motion.

Planting

Prunus cistina, Cotinus coggygria, Berberis, *Rosa rubrifolio,* Tagate, Hemerocallis, and Clematis are seen in **3-58.** Elsewhere are flowering dogwood (*Cornus florida*), *Styrax japonica, Vinca minor,* Azalea, *Euonymus* sp., Buddleia, and Cytisus.

PROJECT 3A

Irregular Bluestone Patio on Stone Dust

YOU WILL NEED
Bluestone of various sizes and shapes, stone dust (or gravel and sand), lump hammer and chisel, two-by-four

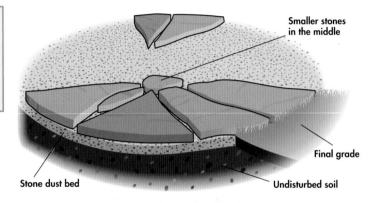

3-59 Irregular stone patio on stone dust.

For home construction, stone on stone dust or in gravel and sand is recommended over stone in cement. In regions that experience heavy frost, there may be occasional heaving, which is easily repaired. Generally, however, if good building techniques are employed, this approach will give you a durable surface with a very pleasing look, relatively inexpensively and without a great deal of work.

Once you have determined the finished grade the stone patio is to have, excavate, if necessary, far enough to allow for several inches of stone dust and the thickness of the stone **(3-59).** Therefore, if you are using 1½-inch-thick stone and your soil drains relatively easily, you will need to excavate 4 to 5 inches. If your soil is hardpan or clay, you should excavate 7½ inches, allowing for a 6-inch bed of stone dust, or several inches of gravel with several inches of stone dust or sand on top.

Stone dust has two very useful and nearly opposing properties. It compacts well, preventing future settling, and it drains **(3-60).** Both of these qualities are a result of it being composed of larger, grit-sized particles and a very fine, dustlike material, both of which are simply ground stone, generally bluestone. In earlier times, we used a sub-base of gravel with sand poured over the top and worked in, and this gave us the same effect. Now stone dust does the job of the gravel and sand; however,

if gravel and sand are more readily available in your area, they will work just fine too. Again, this would be several inches of gravel, compacted, with several inches of sand poured over and packed in with a couple of inches of sand on top into which to set the stones.

Although technically the same as laying a random rectangular bluestone patio, there is an additional, or at least different, aesthetic challenge with the irregular stone patio. When building a patio of random regular-shaped stones—that is, various sizes of rectangles—the aesthetic difficulty lies in creating a pleasing pattern with no long running joints. (This challenge is not there when the stones are all of the same size, as there is no pattern.) With the random rectangular stone patio, the lines of the joints are all straight and there is little difficulty in maintaining consistent joint widths, end to end and side to side.

When the stones are shaped irregularly, however, it is necessary to create a pleasing pattern while maintaining a narrowness of the

97

3-60 A 6-inch bed of stone dust compacts well, preventing future settling, and it drains.

3-61 An attractive patio of irregularly shaped stone, with flowing motion and narrow joints, can almost always be achieved.

3-62 If a stone needs to be made to fit, it a can be shaped with careful hammer-and-chisel work.

joints between the stones. As there are often no straight edges and no consistency of edge line, fitting one stone into the curves of another can be quite difficult. But, as seen in **3-61,** creating an attractive patio of irregularly shaped stones with flowing motion and narrow joints can usually be achieved. The keys are patience, endurance, and holding to a high standard. If the stone you have just spent considerable energy placing doesn't work, take it out and try another. If you keep doing this, you will succeed. As with every kind of stone patio, large pieces should be used on the outside and small pieces on the inside. There should be no small stones at the edge of the patio.

Should you come across a spot where no stone seems to fit well, but one might be made to fit, it's time for the chisel and the lump hammer **(3-62).** Most stones can be shaped with careful hammer-and-chisel work. This isn't easy, and if there is a fracture anywhere in the stone, however subtle, chances are that the stone will break along the fracture, no matter where you hit it or how carefully you bring the chisel and hammer to bear.

To use the chisel, lay the stone where it is to go, determine what needs to be removed, and scratch the line on the stone with the chisel. Set the stone solidly on the earth, sand, or stone dust, with every part of the stone well supported; there should be no gaps beneath. Beginning at one end, place the point of the chisel straight up on the line and give it a sharp hit with the stone or the lump hammer several times. Move the chisel slightly up the line and repeat. Go over the line several times, giving about three firm hits to every chisel placement, following along the line. Some stones respond well to this, and after a few passes along the cut line, you can hit that portion of the stone with the hammer and the piece will break off. Other stones are much harder to cut, and you must continue with the chisel until they begin to break off along the line.

Once the stones are placed in the desired pattern, they must be set. Most flagging stone is flat on one side but not on the other. The bottom side will have many irregularities, and you must fill the voids and scrape away stone dust to receive the protrusions of the bottom surface of the stone. Do this by laying the stone firmly in place, hit it a few times with a rubber mallet, and note where it is high and low in relation to the stones around it. Raise the stone and note the pattern on the stone dust. Where the stone has sat flat against the stone dust will be obvious, and where the stone dust is too low such that the stone did not make contact will also be clear.

Using a mason's trowel and having extra stone dust handy, scrape away the high points, fill the voids, and try again. If it seems to fit, stand on the stone on all its edges. If it wobbles, you have a high point somewhere. Lift the stone and do this again. (It is best to do this with two or three people, as these stones can be quite heavy.) When the stone is finally stable, even with the stones adjacent to it, and at about the right elevation, put a level on it. If it has a significant pitch (and it should not, at

this point), you will need to either raise the low spot or lower the high spot, or do both, being sure it remains even with the adjacent stones.

To level the stone in all directions, use a heavy rubber mallet or, better, a strong 3-foot length of two-by-four on edge. Lay the two-by-four across the stone, and hit the spot on the two-by-four where the stone is high with a heavy lump hammer or a stone hammer. You can use quite a bit of force, because the blow from the hammer is carried the length of the board. (If your stone has a crack, however, it will break.) Move the board all around the stone, hitting it hard repeatedly. This both levels and "sets" the stone. Allow the board to span adjacent stones while you hit it with the hammer. This helps make them level with one another at their edges, avoiding "trip lips."

Bluestone Walk with Belgium-Block Risers

3-63 Bluestone walk with Belgium-block risers.

Constructing the bluestone walk is essentially the same as constructing the bluestone patio on stone dust (Project 3A, page 97 above). Here, we also address the use of Belgium-block risers to create the steps **(3-63).**

In some regions, it will be desirable to set the Belgium block in concrete; however, in many areas where frosts are not severe, the adjacent step will hold the block in place. Belgium block comes in three sizes: small "sets," or cubes, that are 5 x 5 x 5 inches, medium that are 9 x 4 x 5 inches, and jumbo that are 11 x 7 x 5 inches. The jumbo are best to use as risers, as they provide plenty of stone to be set below grade.

The number of risers and their height will be dependent on elevation rise from bottom to top and the number of steps. For outdoor steps, a rise of approximately 5 inches in conjunction with fairly broad steps will provide a comfortable walk with an elegant look.

Beginning at the bottom level, determine the height of the walk and excavate sufficiently for

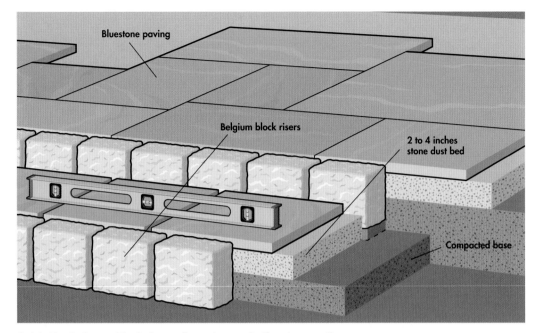

3-64 The Belgium block that will sit about a half inch too tall.

the stone and a base of several inches of stone dust. Lay in the stone dust and the stone, and level (see Chapter 4 Project 4A, page 139). Where the first riser is to be, excavate about 10 inches below the top of the finished grade of the bluestone that will be the bottom step. Fill with 4½ inches of stone dust, and lay in the Belgium block, which will sit about a half inch too tall, or about 5½ inches above the finished walk **(3-64).** Using a heavy hammer or a hammer and a two-by-four, drive the Belgium block into the stone dust to grade—5 inches

above the bottom level of the bluestone. Continue laying in the walk, building the riser, laying in the walk, and so forth, until you have reached the topmost grade.

If you find that the Belgium blocks are driven below the proper level, use more stone dust beneath them until they are set firmly and cannot be driven further into the stone dust bed. Be sure that they are level and that each rise is exactly the same as the others. No set of steps should ever have irregular rises, as this causes people to trip.

Veneer Wall

YOU WILL NEED

Concrete blocks, concrete with reinforcing, bonding agent, anchor tabs, string, plumb, levels, mortar and sand, flat stones of various shapes, brick hammer.

To build a stone-faced veneer wall, it is first necessary to build a concrete-block wall **(3-65)**. This is simply a matter of pouring a reinforced concrete footing and building a block wall on top. For reinforced footings, see Project 2B, "Brick Walk with Mortared Outer Course"on page 54 in Chapter 2.

To build the block wall, allow the footing to have a few days to cure, or use a bonding agent that permits fresh concrete to bond to "green" concrete. String a line from end to end, the height of the first course of block, exactly on the line the wall is to follow, making sure the line is straight and level.

Use one part mortar with three parts sand, mixed to a thick, not runny paste. Lay down a bed of mortar for every course of block, making sure each block is straight, plumb, and level, with a consistent, approximately ½ inch joint between the blocks, end to end and up and down. Use 3-foot and 8-inch levels to check along the length, up and down and side to side.

After each course of block is laid, string a line at the proper height, lay down a bed of mortar, set in the anchor tabs, or ties, and lay down the next course. Always check for the proper line, and be sure that the wall is plumb and level in all directions. Once the wall is built, it can be veneered.

3-65 A concrete-block wall is first necessary for building the veneer wall.

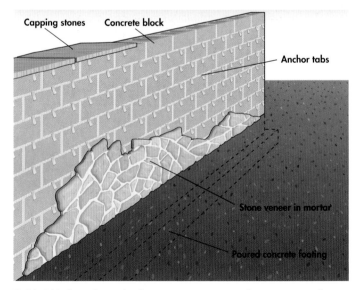

Capping stones   Concrete block

Anchor tabs

Stone veneer in mortar

Poured concrete footing

3-66 Working from the bottom up to create the veneer wall.

3-67 Don't build very high until the mortar beneath has set.

3-68 The wall sweeps from the two bottom outside corners toward the center using the grain of the stones.

There are no real technical difficulties in veneering a block wall. With a trowel, batter up a stone (slap mortar onto the back of a stone, using a mix of one part mortar to three parts sand), working from the bottom up and across **(3-66)**. It is best to hose down the wall first and every now and again, as the block may draw out the moisture of the mortar too fast and a good bond will not be created. Continue on in this fashion, not going very high until the mortar beneath has set **(3-67)**.

Aesthetics, however, are another matter. For some masons, if a stone fits a given space, they will use it there, regardless of its particular qualities. Such construction often results in a wall that is "frozen." The stones' energies all cancel each other out, and the wall has no movement—it appears lifeless.

Other masons prefer to work with the qualities of the stones—their color, grain, and shape—and in so doing can bring about a much more beautiful construction. How you choose to work with the stones' qualities is up to you. In the veneered wall in **3-68,** the grain was used to create sweeping lines from the bottom of both corners up toward the middle. Many other methods for working with the stones were possible, and other stones would offer different options. For example, with less brittle stones, more susceptible to cutting and shaping with a brick hammer, it is possible to work with the form of the stones in creating flowing joint lines. Spend a little time looking at the stone you are working with, noting its qualities, and seeing how you might most effectively bring those qualities out in your construction.

CHAPTER 4

Structure for Delineating Space

Why define separate spaces? Why divide a garden? Basically for the same reasons that we have living rooms and dining rooms, bedrooms and dens—in order to extend the usefulness of the overall space and provide a range of experiences and possibilities.

Often delineating an individual space in the garden is a precursor to creating an area for outdoor living. Instead of simply putting down a patio, building a deck, or creating a place to sit and relax, we might first want to define the space that these areas are to occupy. This will set it apart and provide the comforting effect of seclusion.

Creating different "rooms" also enhances the overall sense of spaciousness of the garden. Two or more garden rooms, each large enough to occupy and use, will always feel larger than the same total space experienced at once. We quickly see the limits of one expanse with no significant divisions, whereas two or more rooms invite us to wander and explore and always leave some things unseen, hinting at what lies beyond.

Hardscape elements are great for achieving this division of space, and the range of options is considerable, from the simple placement of an object, to altering the paving, to the use of arches, arbors, pergolas, and walls. Frequently, several structural elements work together to create spatial delineation. Here, we will begin by looking at individual structural elements used to define space and then move on to more complex projects.

Urbanity Redeemed

One simple device for creating separate areas is an arbor. But it must be used with some thought. Often an arbor will be placed along a walk with nothing distinguishing the spaces on either side. It is just there, and no transition or change occurs in passing through it. Arbors (and this applies to pergolas, gazebos, and similar structures) should not be used simply because we like them or the idea of them. If we do use an arbor for this reason, then we should at least give it a job—we should make it do something for our garden that would not be achieved without it.

In my view, the primary purposes of an arbor are to separate and join two different areas and to create a moment in time when one passes from one into the other **(4-1)**. It is a transition point and a transition moment between two distinct spaces meant for distinct purposes and offering different experiences. Equally as important, to keep it from seeming frivolous, such a structure should seem necessary or even inevitable in its setting.

The original garden was created when the house was constructed about a hundred years ago and was designed for utilitarian purposes **(4-2)**. The tall, steel ladder anchored in concrete, visible in the "before" and "after" images, was used for hanging laundry, while the narrow, concrete walkways maximized the potential for growing vegetables. The new owner had other hopes for it. The ladder could stay, but it would be used to support flowering vines. The concrete would be removed and replaced by a garden that invited outdoor living. In addition, the stairs leading to the garden were modified in such a way that when we arrive at the bottom, we are now standing in the garden and no longer next to the fence. In front of us, on the diagonal, stands this arbor.

Many urban gardens suffer from the same constraints as this one did. They are often exposed, fishbowl-like, to surrounding properties; they are frequently narrow and cramped; and they don't seem to offer much in the way of beauty or pleasure. True to type, this charmless little plot hadn't a lot going for it.

4-1 The arbor creates an entrance into the "dining room." The stairs now leave us standing in the garden, not alongside the fence.

4-2 This is the same view as in 4-1 "before"—cramped and dismal, this property didn't have much going for it.

4-3 The view toward the west side "before."

4-4 The view toward the west side "after."

4-5 Looking from the meditation garden to the "dining room."

Because this garden was so tiny and cramped, dividing it into separate areas might at first seem an unlikely approach to its redemption. This proved otherwise, however. The little wrought-iron arbor dividing the garden into two distinct yet joined areas serves to lift the garden up and out of the ordinary. The arbor offers us two choices: we can either visit the dining area with its ceramic water garden or explore the little meditative garden offering a greater degree of privacy. This example represents, in my view, the minimum differences that should be found between two areas separated by an arbor. The paving is identical, and the planting is the same. But simply by being there, the arbor creates two rooms out of one, and it defines the entrance into the dining area (**4-3** and **4-4**). Although this would have been a pretty garden without the arbor, it provides a definite perception of discreet areas, which helps the garden to appear larger.

While defining space and creating a moment in time as we pass through it, this wrought-iron arbor with its slightly arched top also provides architectural and textural contrast in the garden. The stone and wood planes and the plants all combine wonderfully, but the iron arbor brings out their aliveness and is in turn made more vivid by them. The contrast makes the whole garden "pop." The arbor's placement also establishes the diagonal arrangement of the garden, adding a subtle frisson of energy echoed in the pattern of the bluestone-and-granite paving. The arbor also makes the garden more interesting and inviting and adds a touch of elegance (**4-5**).

4-6 A tub garden brings balance to the plantings and adds another textural quality by virtue of the water.

Scale/Proportion

The arbor was scaled down to a 32-inch width and given a full 7-foot height. This tall, narrow profile helps the garden to seem more ample. Being shorter or wider would have had the opposite effect.

Style

This is a contemporary design—sophisticated in composition, yet warm and earthy in terms of materials—appropriate to the client who commissioned the work.

Additional Hardscape Functions

The arbor brings a touch of *ornamentation* to the garden, particularly through its sharp textural contrast to the surrounding elements, and it *balances* with the

4-7 The far corner. Note the rock among the foliage.

abundant foliage and adds a vertical *dimension*. The lattice fence provides *privacy* without seeming confining and balances pleasantly with the horizontal plane of the paving, which balances texturally with the planting. The cedar lattice is ornamental and becomes more so as flowering vines interweave through it. The random pattern of the bluestone-and-granite paving also creates a pleasing pattern, picked up by the furniture with white squares surrounded by gray. Finally, the stone sculpture tucked within the foliage provides a wonderful contrast, as does the ceramic pot with its water, aquatics, and fish **(4-6** and **4-7).**

Application

In this garden, the arbor is the sole element responsible for creating the effect of two separate but joined rooms. Without it, this would seem like a single space slightly narrower in the center. There are few garden spaces that cannot use an arbor for this effect. Many styles of arbors are available, in a variety of dimensions and materials. The one type of setting in which, in my view, they ought not to be used is along a walk where there is no change or sense of entering another area when passing through.

Planting

The trees are dogwood and weeping redbud (*Cercis canadensis* 'lavender twist' or 'forest pansy'). Around and beneath are Viburnum, Spirea, Hydrangea, juniper, Hosta, *Euonymus fortunei,* Azalea, rose of Sharon (*Hibiscus syriacus*), bleeding heart (*Dicentra spectabilis*), *Vinca minor, Clematis* sp., Wisteria, and Iris.

Victorian Rooms

L ong, relatively narrow sites are among the most receptive areas to the principle of division. By delineating different spaces along them, such sites become less confining and more inviting **(4-8).** In addition, the areas that are created can serve different purposes, offering a greater variety of experiences and pleasures.

4-8 Two divisions create three "rooms," two for use and the other as a visual focal area.

As the "before" image indicates **(4-9),** this garden was fairly featureless and quite unusable—but it had great potential. Long and narrow, it lent itself admirably to division. What, after all, can you do in a space 70 feet by 18 feet? Play boules, perhaps, but these owners were otherwise inclined. In order for this garden to become truly useful for its owners, it needed to be restructured. To work as a visually pleasing environment, it required balancing and harmonizing with the adjacent house **(4-10).**

Delineating spaces in this garden is achieved with two different elements: the arbor, which separates and joins the two primary living spaces, and the low wall, which separates the second living space from the focal dais to the rear of the garden.

The arbor **(4-11)** is made to seem inevitable and necessary by the mature boxwood plantings that extend outward from each side in such a way that passage can take place only through the arbor. The arbor defines the point and moment of transition between the two different areas, each of which offers different uses.

The smaller front garden possesses an informal water garden and soft plantings and is accessed easily from the house by way of a redwood deck with two levels. This space is more intimate and intended for casual use by the family members—it is a place to sit with morning coffee, have a casual meal, or poke about in the garden. As you pass through the arbor, the space opens up on either side and in front of you, revealing a spacious, outdoor room suitable for entertaining larger groups or hosting dinner parties beneath the stars. This room is characterized by formal elements such as an arched wall and geometrical planters with arched fronts, and it is focused on the raised, formally shaped water garden on the elevated dais to the rear **(4-12).** The same paving extends through the two rooms, serving to unify the garden, but because of the arbor, we know when we have left one garden room and entered the other, and this sense of transition is palpable and satisfying.

4-9 Before being redesigned, the garden was divided improperly into unusable spaces.

4-10 In progress—the water garden wall and the retaining wall are in place.

4-11 The arch divides and joins the informal patio with the dining-and-entertaining patio. Beyond lies the raised dais with the focal water garden.

4-12 Repetition of forms in the arch, the retaining wall, the planters, and the water garden helps create unity in the garden.

A FEW THOUGHTS ON
Creating Styles

We often speak of a certain style, such as formal, natural, and so forth. I discuss the style of each project in this book. But I think it is useful to realize that we are not forced to adhere to any known style, as many of the gardens shown here demonstrate. When we create a classical form such as a perfect square or circle or an arch in a natural material like undressed stone, we are blending styles. Often the result can be a creation that is perfectly suited to our own tastes, yet not strictly belonging to any known category.

In addition to delineating spaces, the arbor serves more subtle design functions. Its arch is reflected in the curve of the retaining walls, the planters, and the water garden. Repeating forms in this manner helps bring unity to a garden, allowing for greater diversity without creating chaos. Variety is desirable, but too much variety is disturbing, especially in a small garden. When we achieve a sense of unity through repetition of forms, materials, and textures, diversity can be sustained while maintaining a sense of place. Finally, the arbor serves as ornamentation. Attractive in itself, it is also host to climbing roses, which adds to the overall beauty of the garden.

Note the retaining wall supporting the raised third room. The arch is a classical form and brings a touch

4-13 This retaining wall adds dimension and strength to the garden.

Scale/Proportion

The primary entertaining area is balanced on either end by the small informal patio toward the front, and the raised area with the water garden at the rear. The stone wall on the right is likewise balanced by the stone planters on the left. Each of the elements—the walls, the planters, the arbor, the paving areas and plantings—are of suitable dimensions and, with a combination of elegance, nature, and a touch of the romantic, in all, the spaces seem comfortably proportioned.

Style

This was intended to be suitable to a Victorian-style home.

Additional Hardscape Functions

The rear wall, the stone planters, and the stone wall on the right of the garden also help by their mass and dimensions to *balance* the wall of the home, which would be overpowering if not for these solid structural elements in the garden **(4-13)**. These components also add *dimension* to the garden, lifting it off the horizontal plane into the vertical, and, of course, each has its own *ornamental* value **(4-14)**.

4-14 Looking from the raised dais toward the redwood deck.

of elegance and formality, mitigated by the natural stone and mortarless construction. This wall comfortably embraces and encloses the middle room at that end. The arbor defines the other end of this room, and it serves to focus and highlight the raised, grassy plane behind it, which holds the focal point of the entire garden, the water garden. The rear wall of the water feature repeats the arch of the retaining wall, the planters, and the arbor, gives balance to the leafy planting behind it, and draws the eye through the entire length of the garden.

Application

This approach of dividing a garden to create different rooms is one of the best methods for making the most of long, narrow spaces. In this case, the divisions were along the main axis, but they could have been offset, with equal effectiveness, resulting in a less formal feeling.

Planting

Boxwood (*Buxus sempervirens*), *Cornus sericea, Rhododendron* sp., *Kalmia latifolia, Hydrangea quercifolia,* Berberis, *Vinca minor,* Clematis, roses, Iris, Carex, Liriope, *Cornus kousa,* and climbing hydrangea (*Hydrangea petiolaris*).

Three Pavements,
Three Gardens

Division of space can be very subtle as well as quite simple to achieve. If the aim is to maintain the integrity of a given area and yet hint at a separation and another use, merely altering the paving with some distinguishing element at the point of delineation can do the trick **(4-15** and **4-16)**.

Sometimes we want to introduce variety into a space without losing the expansiveness of the site. We want to have our cake and eat it too. In this garden, the intent was to create livable, usable spaces with a subtle separation, while maintaining the given volume of the site. To achieve this end, a random granite-and-bluestone paving was run abruptly into a paving of granite and Tennessee Crab Orchard **(4-17)**. The water garden placed at the boundary between the two areas but primarily within the second accentuates the separation and indicates another purpose for that space. The larger area to the front of the garden is for family gatherings and dining, whereas the smaller area near the water garden is intended as a quiet, meditative spot **(4-18)**.

Leading off the second area is yet another garden just glimpsed between two Leland cypress trees (*Cupressocyparis lelandii*) **(4-19** and **4-20)**. This is intended as the children's secret garden, replete with its own private entrance, seating area, and fish pond with waterfall. Paving here transforms into gravel, giving the garden an informal, playful feeling **(4-21** and **4-22)**.

Scale/Proportion

Scale is considered in terms of the sizes of the three areas. The second area was intentionally kept small, to contribute to its function as a place for quiet meditation. The primary area is large enough for family gatherings, entertaining, and such. The girls' secret garden is large enough to fool around in, grow a few vegetables, and play around the pond, but small enough to feel private.

4-15 "After"—two garden rooms created by altering the type and the direction of the paving.

4-16 "Before"—an open expanse in need of a garden.

4-17 From above, "after." The paving changes from granite and bluestone to granite and Tennessee Crab Orchard.

4-18 A water garden distinguishes the second area.

4-19 An opening between the Leland cypress hints at another "room."

4-20 Dense planting partially screens the children's secret garden.

4-21 The girls' water garden.

4-22 The secret garden on the left, off the meditation area on the right.

4-23 Planting of both subtle and sharp contrasts and harmonies.

4-24 Stone borders give the garden a natural look.

4-25 "Before"—looking from back to front.

4-26 "After"—from back to front.

Style
Overall, this is a contemporary design mitigated by an organic naturalness, with the secret garden being entirely naturalistic **(4-23** and **4-24)**.

Additional Hardscape Functions
Outdoor living is one of the intents of this garden, and we see it manifesting in all three areas. The curving lines of the planting beds provide a sense of *motion*, as do the water gardens.

Application
The concept of delineating space by varying the pavement can be used in any style of garden and need not introduce a contemporary influence. Even a very organic or naturalistic design can be given this subtle differentiation provided that the materials are suitable **(4-25** and **4-26)**.

Planting
For vertical accents, there are Leland cypress, junipers, dogwood, and *Ilex crenata* 'Sky Pencil.' Also featured here are *Daphne* x *burkwoodii* 'Carol Mackie,' *Deutzia gracillis* 'Nikko,' Hosta, Hydrangea, smoke bush (*Cotinus coggygria*), junipers, Weigela, roses, Carex, Aegopodium, *Vinca minor,* and Heucherella.

Textural Contrasts, Harmonious Forms

In the last project, we dealt with the concept of varying horizontal surfaces to visually delineate space. Here, we continue with that concept to an enhanced degree **(4-27** and **4-28)**.

In the previous example (pages 117 to 122), we saw that simply changing the kinds of paving stones had the effect of defining different spaces. Repeating one kind of stone through two areas helped maintain the quality of unity, while introducing another type of stone provided variety. In this garden, we achieve the same effect by repeating a definite line through entirely different mediums **(4-29)**. This has a similar effect visually as, say, an arbor would physically. In this garden, the lawn, the pebble bed, the water garden **(4-30),** and the perennial border all repeat the same curve of the patio. Here, we may not necessarily pass physically from one area to another, but as the eye travels, the effect is one of traversing over different spaces separated by medium but united through form.

Of course, not much structure is involved in this—just the patio, the water garden, and the pebble bed. The lawn between, interestingly, is integral to the overall effect, in that it provides the greatest contrast between the harder elements and is itself accented by the patio stone and the pebbles.

Scale/Proportion

Scale here is particularly important, as there was very little space with which to work. Neither the lawn area nor the pebble bed could have been any smaller and still be convincing. The patio could have been smaller and not be out of balance with the whole or the other components, but it would have lost its serviceability.

4-27 Before, there were structures delineating space, but not pleasantly so.

4-28 The same view as 4-27, now "after."

4-29 The garden from above—repeating forms through several textures.

4-30 In that it has a definite form outlined by stones, even a small pond provides structural delineation.

Style
This is another contemporary design softened by organic elements. The simple curvilinear motif within the rectilinear framework of the fence contributes to this quality of organic softness. Likewise, the informal planting contributes to this effect.

Additional Hardscape Functions
The lattice fence, which embraces this setting without being confining, provides a vertical accent and an *ornamental* quality, as does the arbor gate **(4-31).**

Application
Gardens large and small can benefit from this approach of breaking up a space visually while maintaining a continuous plane. Large expanses, however, lend

4-31 The grape arbor gate leads to the neighbor's property.

themselves especially to this treatment. Public spaces come to mind. They are often paved with one continuous material, when some variation would have been enlivening and appreciated.

Planting

Miscanthus sinensis 'Gracillimus' and *Rosa rubrifolia* edge the patio. Near the grape arbor, Caryopteris and Hydrangea thrive. Around the pool are ferns, Daphne, Spirea, Hosta, Carex, and a dwarf hemlock (*Tsuga canadensis 'Coles Prostrate'*).

Reflecting Pools with a View

There are times when a single expanse of space is desirable—when we want to generate a sense of grandness or magnitude, for example. More often, though, we derive more enjoyment and serviceability when we divide a space into areas adaptable to everyday use. And sometimes we can have both **(4-32).**

As the "before" image shows **(4-33),** this area just outside the house afforded a wonderful view but possessed no hardscaped space or living area from which to enjoy it. This area could have been designed as one elevation—a large patio, say, with a retaining wall on the far side. But the possibility of several levels stepping down to a final lookout terrace offered more dramatic interest and promised to be more fun **(4-34).**

There are a variety of places to relax and dine. One can even stroll, glass of champagne in hand, beneath the pergolas to the lower terrace, while enjoying the shimmering images in the reflecting pools and the scenic view beyond.

As is often the case, several hardscape elements work together here to delineate the various areas. The steps from the main patio join at the next level, accentuated by the periodic cascade of water down to the reflecting pool **(4-35).** Another flight of steps and two pergolas lead to the lower level, accented by its own small reflecting pool. Together, these structures define three open, interconnected rooms, each with its own qualities and vistas **(4-36).**

Scale/Proportion

The entire paved area easily accommodates about fifty guests. The upper patio comfortably seats twelve to fourteen; the lowest level can seat ten to twelve. The middle area is meant as a passage between and is wide enough for two abreast. The main pool is large enough to reflect a portion of sky without dominating the space. The lower pool might have been made larger but for fear of taking away too much space in which to congregate, as this is a destination area with the best view. The pergolas seem well scaled to the space. Although they might have been made a little lower, their being taller would not have worked.

4-32 One space was divided into three.

4-33 "Before," with no comfortable space from which to enjoy the grand view.

4-34 The upper patio provides ample space for dining and entertaining.

4-35 When the system is on, water cascades over the steps into the pool.

4-36 The lower terrace has its own reflecting pool.

4-37 Ornamental grasses soften the structural elements.

Style

This is a classically formal design, symmetrically balanced down the long axis, with just a hint of a contemporary feel **(4-37)**.

Additional Hardscape Functions

Clearly, *outdoor living* is invited here, and the pools and pergolas possess an *ornamental* quality.

Application

Not every property could sustain so much formal structure or would be suitable for this degree of elegance. Where there is ample space and where architecture and taste run to the formal, such a design will work.

Planting

Various ornamental grasses, lavender, roses, and arborvitae, with highlights of *Cornus alba*, constitute the majority of plants here. A white Wisteria climbs up one pergola, a purple Wisteria up the other.

Susan's Place

When we consider all the acres of suburban and rural land devoted to expanses of open lawn, we realize that imagination and a little work could make such a difference. A bench here, a little paving there, a table, an arbor, a small pool—and everywhere plants—is all it would take to make these lawns into wonderlands. Well, we must wonder why this isn't done more.

We first visited this garden in Chapter 3, Structure for Instilling Motion, as we followed the winding brick path past copious plantings. Here, we will visit the various garden rooms to which that path leads and by which this landscape is embellished **(4-38).**

There isn't anything especially complicated about this garden, but there is certainly something wonderful about it. Fairly good sized for a town lot, it seems

4-38 From the open porch, the garden exhibits a variety of places to view and to visit.

4-39 An informal patio provides seating amidst a plethora of flowering perennials.

nearly endless because of all the vistas and spaces created by the casual yet careful placement of various structural elements.

Looking out from the open porch, we glimpse a bench and a patio off to the left, an arbor beyond that, and to the right what appears to be the edge of a pond with river stones. It is pleasant to wander through a well-made garden, but all the more so when in our roaming we see structures that beckon us and come to places that seem to be awaiting our arrival.

This casual patio, for example, offers a place to rest and enjoy the views of the immediate garden **(4-39).** Beyond is another paved area with a birdbath, and past that, the arbor invites us to explore further **(4-40).**

Similarly, walking down the brick path, we find a small bench and table, defining a little space that breaks the longer walk into two short walks and providing a place to sit and enjoy the water garden **(4-41).** We also see from here other areas of the garden awaiting our appreciation **(4-42).**

4-40 From the patio, other garden rooms beckon.

4-41 The koi pond.

4-42 From this little seating area, other garden rooms can be glimpsed.

4-43 Further along the path awaits another seating area with its own views.

4-44 From beneath the grape arbor, another informal patio sweeps into the center of the garden.

4-45 Looking back to the house.

4-46 The center of the garden, paved in marble and with a central birdbath.

Further along, the walk widens into another free-form patio, covered over with a grape arbor with a small table and chairs beneath **(4-43)**. Now another potentially unused space has become a pleasant destination with its own uses, offering more views of the garden **(4-44)**. And note, it didn't take much—a table and chairs by a planter box—and a garden room was created. The grape arbor provides the shade.

This patio sweeps away toward the iron arbor, seen from the front of the garden. Through two junipers, we find our way to the little area spied earlier, with its marble paving and central birdbath, and the circuit is complete **(4-45, 4-46)**.

A FEW THOUGHTS ON
Scaling Up, Scaling Down

It would be reasonable to think that considerable space would be required to have a walkway, a stone patio, a brick patio, a water garden with a seating area, an herb garden and another seating area, and an abundance of plants, but as this garden shows, that is not so. A space half this size could have these same elements—simply scaled down. A water garden would be as effective on a smaller scale, as would an herb garden and a patio. When we see everything in scale to everything else, each element has its own validity and the space as a whole looks correct and complete.

Scale/Proportion

Because no one area was made too large, a variety of garden rooms was possible, each serving its own purposes. The area of marble paving with the birdbath might have been made a little wider, but that space is meant only as a transition between two larger rooms and to showcase the lovely plantings.

Style

This garden is relaxed and casual, with ornamental elements. Although it is a town garden, it has a style I can only classify as "rural elegant."

Additional Hardscape Functions

Outdoor-living possibilities abound, *ornamentation* is found throughout, and, as discussed in Chapter 3, there is a great deal of *motion*.

Application

Almost all yards and gardens can contain a variety of different spaces delineated though simple or complex structures, and most would benefit from having them.

Planting

Near the stone patio: Stokesia, pink geraniums, pink Monarda, Hosta, *Perovskia atriplicifolia*, *Aruncus dioicus*, bachelor buttons, Artemisia, Platycodon, Iris, Shasta daisies

Near the brick patio: Lythrum, lilies, bee balm, yarrow, Hemerocallis, Artemisia, Shasta daisies, foxglove, *Geranium*, Rudbeckia, Iris, tree peony, Coreopsis

Near the birdbath: Delphinium, Phlox, thyme, rosemary, *Geranium,* sage, parsley, lemon balm, bee balm, asters, tarragon

Random, Rectangular Bluestone on Stone Dust

Bluestone and other regular, random, rectangular paving stones come in 6-inch increments. So, there are 12" x 12" stones, 18" x 24" stones, and so forth. However, a nominal 12-inch stone is really 11.5 inches, a nominal 24-inch stone is really 23.5 inches, and so on. This allows for a half-inch joint between stones, primarily for when they are being set in mortar. If they are not set in mortar, you can either maintain a joint between the stones or run the stones up against one another. Both work, but take into consideration what you are going to do when figuring your measurements. If you want to plant between the stones with grass or moss or some groundcover you can walk on, make the joint at least an inch wide. Stones tend to get hot and will burn the roots of anything planted between if the stones are too close.

When I work with random, rectangular bluestone, I like to purchase about five to seven different sizes in different quantities. For a 125-square-foot patio, I might use four pieces 12" x 12", five pieces 12" x 18", five pieces 18" x 18", six pieces 24" x 18", seven pieces 24" x 24", five pieces 24" x 30", and five pieces 30" x 30". For a larger patio, my larger pieces

would be 30" x 36" and 36" x 36", but there would be few of them. This is not a formula and there are countless variations, but using a good mix gives the most satisfying results and provides for the odd stone to get you out of an odd corner without cutting.

Before laying the patio, create the bed (see Project 3A, "Irregular Bluestone Patio on Stone Dust" on page 97). Fill your excavated area with stone dust and rake it level. You can place a 3- or 4-foot level across a length of two-by-four to get your level, or you can use a string level. With the string level, put four stakes inside the bed and string a line between the opposite pairs. Put a line level on the strings, and note the elevation differences of the stone dust bed. Adjust by raking the stone dust into or out of place as needed. You don't need exact level here, only as close as each stone will need to be set individually, but if you get a flat, level bed, the rest is easier. Once this is accomplished, you will be ready to build a patio, but first a word on drainage and pitch.

Most stone patios of this sort, in most locations, such as a backyard, do not need to be pitched, even when they are close to the house. This is because they do not hold water. The water drains between the stones and straight down, just as if it were ground. If you do not already have a water problem in your house, a properly laid stone patio on stone dust will not create one. Where there is a drainage problem, or if the patio is being built on concrete, there should be both a slight pitch away from the house and possibly a drain as well.

When laying out the stone, you want to be aware of several factors. There are random patterns that can result from using different-sized stones, some more attractive than others, and it is good to have an eye to this all the way through construction. After I have laid a couple of stones and I like how they look together, I scratch what I want to see in the stone dust and look for the stone(s) that will give me that pattern.

Avoid long, continuous joints, as they look weak, unless you are creating a definite, symmetrical pattern that calls for this. In random work, break the joint every couple of stones by laying a stone across the joint line. Have some of your stones run along one axis, and balance by laying others on the other axis. It need not be an even balance, however. Stand back every so often and look it over. The pattern should be pleasing. There should not be too many large stones in one area, with a preponderance of small stones nearby, for example. A dynamic balance is the goal.

Never use the smaller stones on the outside, whether doing cement work or on stone dust, as this will both look and be weak. Use your smaller stones to lighten up the inside and to bring an element of detail or even delicacy to the construction **(4-47)**. Use your large stones on the outside, in key places and where there is the heaviest traffic.

Another factor to be aware of is consistency of line. If you have, for example, laid your patio with one axis parallel to your home and the other perpendicular, stand back during construction every now and again and make sure you have remained true to course. It is very easy while immersed in the details to lose sight of the larger picture. Check it from key vantage points as well, such as the main room looking out onto the patio or from where it will often be approached.

If you find yourself needing to cut a stone to fit, there are two tools available. Both are

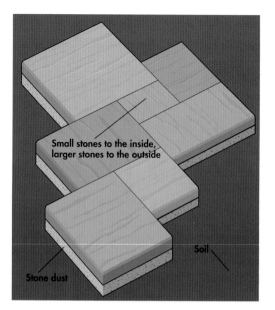

4-47 For the random, rectangular bluestone on stone dust, use your smaller stones to lighten up the inside.

quite serious machines and must be used with extreme caution. One is the "chop saw"— a gas-powered machine with a large blade. The other is an angle grinder, which is much smaller. The latter is my choice, with a diamond-tip blade.

For the best look, mark the stone on the bottom where the cut needs to be and cut along the line most of the way through the stone. Lay it on its bottom and hit the cut portion with a rubber mallet. It will snap off, leaving a snapped-off edge rather than a cut edge.

Note that these are serious tools—they are not for amateurs and should not be used without proper knowledge, skill, clothing, and equipment, including goggles.

Flexible-Liner Pond

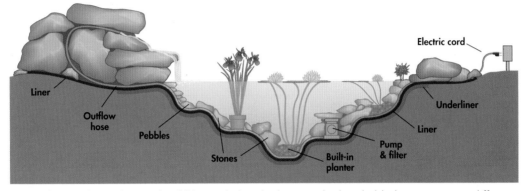

Electric cord

Liner

Outflow hose

Pebbles

Stones

Built-in planter

Pump & filter

Liner

Underliner

4-48 The pond you design should have shelves built into it, both to hold plants in pots at different levels and to receive the stone, which will improve the aesthetics of the pond.

YOU WILL NEED
Garden hose and/or powdered chalk, lime, or marking paint, plants in pots, cat litter or sand mixed with soil, liner and underliner (as desired), stones, pebbles, pump and filter, hose

Once the site has been determined, the pool must be designed on the ground. Many people use a garden hose to lay out the shape, but powdered chalk, bagged lime, or marking paint, available at many building supply and hardware stores, work well too. Remember when drawing the intended pool shape on the ground, to make it about a foot wider and longer (and a little deeper) than the body of water that you wish to see, because space will be taken up by the materials. Also, exaggerate the curves. They tend to flatten out in construction.

The hole that you excavate should have shelves built into it, both to hold plants in pots, should you decide to use pots at different levels, and to receive the stone, which will help with the aesthetics of the pond. Creating shelves shortens the vertical planes within the water garden, which makes them easier to cover in stone **(4-48).** If you were to make the pool with no shelves, the side of the pool would be as tall as the pool is deep and covering that with stone is problematic.

To create the excavation, it is usually recommended that you begin from the deepest part and work outward. Another approach is to excavate the outside line to approximately ½ foot and then continue from the center outward, switching back and forth. Make the shelves as level as possible, or pitch them up slightly toward the outside edge, and make them wide enough to accommodate pots and stones, at least 8 inches. This makes it easy for plants in pots to be set on them without falling over. Make the vertical sides of the shelves as short as possible so that the liner is easily hidden by fewer and smaller stones. The depth should be such that the water does not freeze to the bottom. With 6 inches to a foot of water, fish will survive beneath the ice, and during winter, require no feeding.

An alternative to placing potted plants on shelves is to create depressions in the soil during excavation and then add cat litter or sand mixed with soil to those depressions once the liner is in place. These holes are then planted and covered with small river stones before the pool is filled with water, once construction is done. The plants themselves will then tend to grow over and cover the liner.

One of the easiest mistakes to make in digging the pond is not to provide adequate space for the pump. There are three factors to consider in this regard:

Water recirculation—it is best to have the pump on the opposite side of the pond as that of the waterfall or return line, in order to provide maximum circulation and aeration of the water.

Visibility—neither the pump nor its electric cord or return hose should be seen.

Accessibility—the pump should be removed easily.

This means that wherever you place the pump (on a shelf or in a depression created for that purpose), be sure to wrap sufficient electric cord and water line around it so that the pump/filter can be removed completely and easily for rinsing.

When you have finished the excavation, check the elevations with a level set on top of a two-by-four or a string line level, to make sure all the edges of the pond are level with one another. A low point will determine the water level, and anything above that point will show as raised wall—and this is usually unsightly. If there is a low point, add soil to that edge or lower the other edges. Remove any stones or large roots from the excavation.

Lining the Pond

To determine what size of liner to use, measure the length of the two walls and the bottom along one axis and add 2 feet. Do the same for the other axis. If you determine that you need, for example, a liner that is 12 feet by 15 feet, including the 2 extra feet you added to each axis, then that would be what most sources would tell you to order. There are those, however, who, in the same instances, would purchase a liner that is 15 feet by 20 feet. This is a consequence of having frequently decided in the course of construction to change the shape of or add more depth to a pond. It can be extremely frustrating to find you are an inch shy of enough material to complete the pool as you would like it. Although you can bind liner to liner, this is neither easy nor convenient to do, especially once it is in place. When determining the size of the liner, you'll also want to allow for extra material in the vicinity of the waterfall. This is explained a bit further on.

Before placing the liner in the excavation, it is generally wise to use an underliner, supplied by the same sources that sell liners. This is a feltlike material that is effective in preventing punctures from small stones and such. It is inexpensive, can be purchased in square-foot sheets or by the roll, and is also useful in placing under stones, on top of the liner. To lay it in, cut a piece to the right size, lay it over the excavation, and drop it in. As an aside: It is ten times easier to build a pond with four hands than with two. With a helper, you can, for example, position the underliner and the liner over the pond and drop them right in. Alone, you will have to drag them over, often knocking debris into the excavation and breaking away your neatly excavated walls. Ponds can be built by oneself, but having help is always better.

One person should work from the middle inside, and the other on the outside. Work all away around the pool in one direction, getting the underliner to lay as flat as possible against all surfaces and folding it into pleats where it appears natural to do so.

When the underliner is as flat as it will get, drop in the liner. Then carefully get down in there (you might want to do this in your socks or with felt tied around your boots) and fold the liner into pleats as you did the underliner.

Try not to step on the edges of your shelves, as they break easily, making placement of the pots later on difficult or impossible. Be sure you have sufficient liner material all around the outside edges of your excavation with 2 feet or more where you plan to have the waterfall.

Fill the hole with water. As it fills, the liner will be pulled into the hole, filling the voids. If you have some sides shorter than others, place stones along these edges, allowing the liner to be pulled into the hole from the other sides. It is best to let the pond, once filled, sit for an hour or even overnight, to be absolutely certain there are no leaks. Mark the water level before you leave, and then note if there is any decline. Once you are convinced that the integrity of the liner has not been compromised, you can begin the real work—making the water garden look good, and to do this, you will want to drain the pond. But a word of caution first: At this point, you see where the edges of your pond are going to be and there is a real temptation to cut off the excess liner. Don't. Many a pond builder has been certain where the pond should end, cut away the liner, and later regretted this. Let the last thing you do be the removal of what you will then know beyond all doubt is excess liner—and even then, don't do it. Bury it instead, for potential future use.

Stoning the Pond

Once the flexible or rigid liner is in place, the aesthetic work of placing the river stone begins. This will rarely look absolutely natural, but it can look quite good if the right stones are used and some aesthetic sensitivity employed in their placement **(4-49).** The stones in the pond should be water-worn, smooth with rounded edges, referred to as "river rock," "river flats," or "'river rounds." The stones outside do not need to be water-worn but should not be too dissimilar from the river rocks. Use larger stones against the vertical surfaces and smaller stones and river pebbles on the horizontal surface. Try not to stack them, but place them so that the larger ones are on the bottom, naturally supporting the smaller stones above. The combination of these varying sizes, along with the water and the margin plants, will help create a natural, pleasing look.

Be sure to cover all unnatural elements, such as the cords, the water lines, and the pump and filter, with the stones. Make sure, however, that you have left enough hose and electric line with the pump and filter and that they are placed so that they can be lifted from the pond for cleaning.

If you don't want to see plastic or clay pots in your pond, you can build planters with the

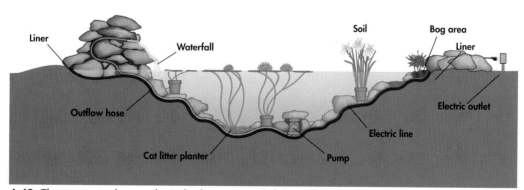

4-49 The stones in the pond can look quite good if the right stones are used and placed with an aesthetic eye.

river stones, cementing them together in pleasing shapes. These will blend into the pond bottom and sides. If you build them at different elevations, they will provide excellent, permanent planting places for all your aquatics. Once the inside of the pond has been covered with stones, you can make the outside of the pond look good with stone too, but try to avoid a necklace of stones around the perimeter of the pond. If possible, extend the stonework to surrounding areas and build in planting pockets.

CHAPTER 5

Structure for Creating Focal Points

Focal points perform a function similar to that of structural elements used for balance, as explored in the first chapter. A structural element placed to give relief from—to provide balance against—an abundance of leaves and flowers offers a place of visual rest; it is an island of solidity within a sea of foliage. A focal point goes one step further. It offers not just solidity, but a port-of-call to the wandering eye adrift within a sea of vegetation or an unvarying expanse. Just as solid elements provide mass and textural balance, a focal point gives directional balance and can serve as an orientation point for an entire setting. In the purest sense, a focal point is a device used to orient us in the garden and to awaken our consciousness to it, and as such, is not a necessary element in every garden. Many gardens have other means of drawing our awareness into them.

Occasionally, an arbitrary placement of a focal element can be effective, especially in a very unstructured setting. More commonly, focal points are placed at the termination of an axis, drawing us along the length of a visual or actual path. We also frequently find them placed in a central location, in which case the surrounding compositional elements, such as planting beds, are focused on the focal point, thus serving to direct our attention.

Attention is the operative word here. The more esoteric function of a focal point is to perk up our attention to bring us more fully into the garden by bringing *us* into focus or helping us focus. To perform this fairly lofty task, the focal point must not be confusingly complex nor can it be uninteresting. If confusing, it will not focus but distract us. If lacking interest, our attention will wander. Here, we look at a variety of hardscape elements used as focal points in the garden. Rather than presenting an in-depth analysis of individual garden projects, we will discuss the different classes of focal points—terminal, central, and arbitrary.

Terminal Focal Points

There is something compelling about an object at the end of a long view or allée awaiting us. Invariably, we feel drawn onward; although we can see what it is that we are approaching, we are not content until we arrive.

Without the awaiting pergola, the walkway in **5-1** would be pleasant but somehow lacking meaning. The pergola lets us know that we are going somewhere, and when we get there, we will be someplace special.

The same is true of the two gardens in **5-2** and **5-3.** Our attention goes out to these objects and focuses on them. They draw us forward, and as with the last garden, they establish for us a meaning to the walkway and a reason for us to be walking on it. This is quite a remarkable effect for a simple object to produce—a consequence of placement and the balancing effect of structure, as discussed in the first chapter.

5-1 A pergola awaits our arrival and gives meaning to our journey.

5-2 An allée with a destination and a reason for being.

5-3 The focal point pulls our attention within the garden, drawing us forward.

The bench in the garden in **5-4** is a less effective enticement, and it is easy to see why. The axis that leads toward it is interrupted by steps along the way. Although it is placed centrally to the arch and the pathway leading to it, there is not the imperative of arrival experienced in the other gardens. Our focus is not continuous, owing to the distracting interference. We don't "lock in" and are not compelled to advance.

Something similar happens in the garden in **5-5.** There is a focal point at the extreme end of this allée and one in the middle, but neither draws us forward. This seems to be because of the sculpted balls that occupy the four corners of this space. They, in conjunction with the central focal structure, create equilibrium—a stasis that inhibits movement. If the front two were removed, the central figure were not there, or the far element were much larger, we would feel more of a compulsion to approach the distant focal point. It is likely that the intent here was to effect a balance, thereby creating a scene meant to be viewed rather than explored.

5-4 An interrupted avenue to a focal point is less compelling.

5-5 Though there is a focal point in the distance, we are not compelled forward.

5-6 The focal point lends dignity and sustains our attention.

The long reflecting pool with the focal urn in **5-6** underscores both primary functions of a focal point: imparting importance and focusing our attention. If you cover the urn, say, with a piece of paper, it becomes immediately evident that as elegant as this reflecting pool is, the urn bestows upon it a degree of dignity that would otherwise be lacking. We also experience the phenomenon that because of the urn, we want to continue looking at this scene. The pool without the urn quickly becomes commonplace and our attention flags. With the urn, this garden remains magical and we delight in viewing the urn, the pool, and the reflection of the urn in the pool. The focal element gathers our attention, refocuses us, and encourages a sustained enjoyment of the garden, just as the structural elements discussed in the first chapter refresh our eye and permit a prolonged appreciation of the plantings.

Scale/Proportion

For focal points to be effective, they must be in scale with the setting they occupy. If too small, their impact is diminished and their function lost; if too large, they can be absurd and overpowering. In the first five examples of terminal focal points, each is well scaled in the setting it occupies, particularly the first and third examples. It is tempting to think that the urn at the end of the pool in **5-6** could have been a little smaller, but the impact it has is so satisfying I think it is best the way it is. In the example in **5-2**, the urn on the pedestal seems to be at the upper limit—meaning, if it were any larger, it wouldn't work—but it could have been smaller and still been effective.

In the example in **5-6,** the wide allée through an orchard with the marble balls, the focal element at the far end could have been much larger, had the intent been to draw us onward, and would then have been more compelling **(5-7).**

Style

As with scale, the style of the focal element should be in harmony with its setting. A contrasting style will detract from the setting as a whole, destroying the quality of unity. Again, each of the focal elements presented here seems well suited to its environment, contributing to the overall impact of the garden.

Additional Hardscape Functions

There is an *ornamental* aspect to each of the focal elements, they generally provide *balance* with the foliage, and they all add another *dimension* to the garden.

Application

All the focal points in these examples were placed at the terminus of a walk or allée, with the exception of the stone urn that is at the end of a long, narrow pool. The approach leading to the focal point has a strong bearing on its impact.

5-7 A larger focal point at the end of this allée would have been more compelling.

To create the sort of effect these focal points have, it is therefore necessary to generate a sense of a restricted, definite, and straight avenue toward the focal element. However, there are other ways and methods of using a focal point, as discussed in the following sections.

Planting

5-1: *Salvia* x 'Blue Queen,' *Campanula glomerata,* Dianthus, *Alchemilla mollis, Stachys byzantina,* Eryngium, Ligularia, *Heliopsis helianthoides, Allium senescens,* Glaucum, *Euphorbia polychroma*

5-2: *Clematis* x 'Perle d'Azur,' *Wisteria sinensis,* roses, Taxus

5-3: *Clematis* x 'The President,' *Rosa banksii 'Lutea,' Fatsia japonica,* Hosta, *Magnolia liliflora 'Nigra'*

5-4: Yew, red and white valerian, Artemisia, *Alchemilla mollis, Crambe cordifolia*

5-5: Apple orchard

5-6: *Carpinus Betulus 'Columnaris,'* Impatiens, water lily (*Nymphaea* x)

Central Focal Points

The next category is the central focal point around which various elements are usually oriented. Central focal points are often less dramatic than terminus focal points, but can be equally as effective in gathering and focusing our attention, elevating our presence in the garden. Like terminal focal points, they also serve to bring meaning to the settings in which they are placed and usually provide balance as well.

In the garden in **5-8,** we have both a terminal focal point, the bench, and a central focal point, the pool. It is the central focal point that is under consideration here. This is a symmetrical arrangement with pairs of elements balanced around the centerpiece. It is the distribution of elements around the central point that gives the central element its power. They are focused on it, and because of that, we focus on it as well. As the central element to which everything else is referring,

5-8 A central fountain with pairs of elements oriented toward it draws and focuses our attention.

5-9 This central focal point is effective in creating balance and adding dimensionality, but because of the abundant plantings, it only partially focuses our attention.

5-10 The focal point loses some of its effectiveness when our attention is drawn away to the abundant flowering perennials.

it becomes the object of our attention, heightening our awareness and bringing us more consciously into the garden. This is the ultimate function that a focal point can serve—to raise our level of consciousness in the apprehension of beauty. And, naturally, the more beautiful the garden and its elements are, the more profound is our experience and the more elevated is our consciousness.

The very pretty garden in **5-9** also contains a central focal point, but it is not as effective as that in the last garden. The reason for this is that though all the beds are focused toward the central element, they are planted so lushly and eclectically that there is no sense of orientation toward the center. As a result, the focal point does not have nearly the focusing power as in the last garden and serves more the function of balance, which it does well.

The same can be said of the formally arranged perennial garden in **5-10,** with its central fountain. Everything does orient toward the focal point, but much of our attention is drawn to the bountiful flowers and we do not have the sense of focusing toward the fountain **(5-11).** Consequently, it is less gripping as a focal point and serves more to balance with the abundant perennials.

The central focal point in the garden in **5-12,** our last example, is more or less central to an axial arrangement and definitely has the attention-focusing effect of that in the first garden in this category. As for my own taste, the form from which the water emerges is both too complex and inappropriate for the otherwise controlled design and planting of the entire setting. This, for me, creates a lack of harmony such that the focal point attracts and focuses but does not please. No doubt, this is a matter of taste, and for anyone liking the design of the fountain, this would be equally as effective a focal point as any shown here.

Scale/Proportion

The first, second, and third of these central focal points seem well scaled to their environment, though the second could be larger given the abundant foliage surrounding it. The last could be a little smaller.

Style

5-8: Formal in arrangement, but softened considerably by the planting

5-9: Similar to the previous example, with a cloister garden feel

5-10 and **5-11:** Again, the arrangement is formal, yet the profusion of blossoms conveys more of a cottage garden style

5-12: The arrangement is contemporary formal, the planting asymmetrical

5-11 The central fountain serves more to balance with the abundant perennials than to be the focal point.

5-12 A focal point out of harmony with its surroundings.

Additional Hardscape Functions

As with the previous category of focal points, these help to *balance* with the foliage and add *dimensionality* and *ornamentation*.

Application

Central focal points work best where surrounding elements can be balanced around and oriented toward them. This generates symmetry and tends to lend a formal or classical element, so they work best where a formal design is suitable.

Planting

5-8: Boxwood with yews beside the bench, grapes in pots, *Stipa gigantea*, Mimulus

5-9: *Thymus* sp., *Stachys byzantina*, *Sedum 'Vera Jameson,'* winter savory, hyssop, sage, *Allium* sp., lemon balm

5-10 and **5-11:** Hemerocallis, Lilium, *Monarda didyma*, Delphinium, *Sedum* sp., *Allium* sp., Iris, Dianthus, Coreopsis

5-12: *Buxus sempervirens, Acer palmatum, Magnolia soulangeana*, Pulmonaria

Arbitrary Focal Points

By arbitrary, I simply mean not belonging to the previous two categories—not at the end of an axis nor central to an arrangement. For the arbitrary focal element to be effective, it must be more dramatic than either of the other types simply because there will be nothing else in the landscape that forces our attention toward it. It has a harder job, so to speak.

This dramatically planted terra-cotta pot is a case in point. Placed within a bed, neither at the end nor at the center of anything, it still commands our attention quite effectively **(5-13)**. The pot itself seems to leap out from the surrounding foliage, but the bold flourish of the variegated Yucca demands that we focus before surveying the surrounding garden.

In this next garden, we find an exception to a rule. Generally, for a focal point to be effective, it should be solitary, or else our attention is divided between objects and tends to dissipate. In the garden seen in both **5-14** and **5-15,** the stone sculpture and the burnished-steel egret work together to fix us in space and time. The moment we come upon this scene, we snap out of our dream and focus on where we are.

Additional Hardscape Functions

5-13: *Balance*

5-14 and 5-15: *Balance* and *ornamentation*

Application

Loosely structured or asymmetrical spaces lend themselves to the arbitrary focal point.

Planting

5-13: *Cordyline australis*, roses, Ceanothus, *Hosta undulata, Zantedeschia aethiopica*

5-14 and 5-15: Native ferns, *Acer palmatum,* Iris

A FEW THOUGHTS ON
Things in Settings

Generally, it seems, the less structured the setting (for example, woods or a very eclectic and lush planting), the more hard items or arbitrary focal elements can be used effectively. It can be quite pleasantly awakening to wander down a woodsy path and come to a series of focal elements embedded within the surrounding foliage. Not only do they provide us with the pleasure of balance and focus, but they also let us know that something intentional (and friendly, I hope) has been done here.

5-13 Arbitrary placement of a focal point requires that the element be more dramatic in order to gain and focus our attention.

5-14 The egret with its glittering eye holds our attention.

5-15 An exception to a rule, two focal points in this natural landscape serve to focus us in the space and time.

Formal Fountain

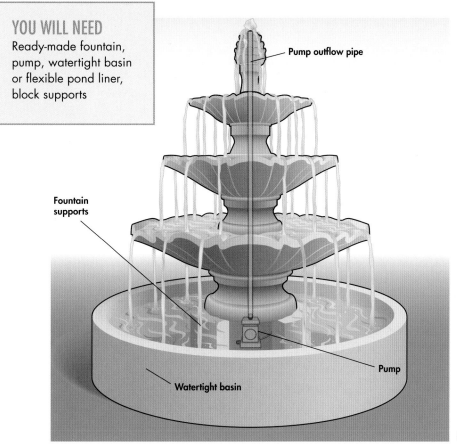

Pump outflow pipe

Fountain
supports

Pump

Watertight basin

5-16 Formal fountain.

A formal fountain is characterized by symmetry and the basin design is typically uncomplicated—a rectangle or circle. This structure is a highly visual phenomenon and should be located where it will have the greatest impact—often in the center of a space, or centered on one axis but not the other.

Formal fountains normally come already plumbed. Installation involves attaching a pump at the bottom to the outflow tube that runs up through the fountain and making sure the fountain and pump are situated within a watertight basin **(5-16)**. Place blocks for the fountain to sit on. In addition the electric line from the pump needs to be run over the walls to the power source.

If there is no preconstructed basin, excavate and line with a flexible pond liner, installed in a manner similar to Project 4B, "Flexible-Liner Pond," pages 141 to 144. In excavating, keep your measurements exact and, if the basin is a rectangle, keep the walls square. If you are using stone, save time and work by making the dimensions correspond to the measurements of the stone. The electric line should go under, not over, the stone that is to line the pool walls. If there is to be no final finishing material, such as stone, it is a good idea to have a liner made to exact dimensions along with hardware for securing the corners.

Self-Contained Wall Fountain

Wall fountain with pump, drill with masonry bit, masonry anchor bolts or screws

Generally, wall fountains are placed on existing walls. The self-contained types are quite easy to install and make excellent focal points. Like the standing fountain, the self-contained wall fountain comes plumbed already and is usually sold with a pump attached **(5-17).** The pump sits in the bottom basin. A rubber hose attaches to an outflow tube that goes to the outflow device—a rosette, the mouth of a lion, or whatever.

If attaching to a masonry wall, it is necessary to drill the wall first with a masonry bit. To do so, have the unit held where it is to go and mark where the holes will be. Drill the wall and secure the fountain with either masonry anchor bolts or masonry screws, depending on the weight of the fountain. Run the electric cord to a switched outlet, fill the basin with water, and turn it on.

Fountain

Water line between fountain and wall

First spill basin

Second spill basin with pump

Electric line between fountain and wall

5-17 Wall fountain in one piece.

CHAPTER 6

Structure for Creating Privacy

As with focal points, and not like balance and dimension, privacy is not essential to the success or enjoyment of every garden. Many gardens are private simply because of a fence or a lack of neighbors. Some gardens are meant to be seen and not used; others are exposed, but the manner in which they are used makes that exposure immaterial, so privacy isn't an issue.

However, for many gardens and gardeners, privacy is an important consideration **(6-1).** For example, those living in urban areas, surrounded by curious onlookers, often crave privacy in their gardens. Even in suburban or rural areas, where children run free or a neighbor might drop by at any time, the quality of privacy can be desirable. And then, there is simply the natural impulse to "get away," to be alone sometimes, to read a book out in the fresh air, to think, just to be. There is something warm and delicious about being outside, in a natural setting with the sense of having escaped, that drives us to the furthest corners of our gardens. In this chapter, we look at a few structures designed for creating just this sense of privacy.

Creating a Private Place

As these next two gardens demonstrate, not much space is required to create a private place, and if some corner doesn't lend itself to a little seclusion, you can always make it so that it does. Two panels of lattice at right angles may be all that it takes **(6-1)**. For a cozy corner, add a pergola, some paving, and a table and chairs **(6-2)**. Even without the overhead structure, this corner provides ample privacy in a very small area.

In the garden seen in **6-3,** we find the same concept extended to include a larger space. It still provides privacy, but with a more expansive feeling of space. This too consists only of lattice panels with overhead beams for vines and shade, light paving, and a table and chairs.

6-1 Simply screening off a section of the garden with lattice panels affords a pleasant sense of privacy.

6-2 Two lattice panels and a table and two chairs create a cozy corner.

6-3 An ornate pergola creates a romantic haven.

Both settings contain considerable ornamentation—particularly this last one, which for some would be a bit overpowering, with its abundant, brilliant hanging baskets, rose-red posts and beams, variegated foliage, and the sculpture of lovers seen through the ornate window. Adding to the complexity here is the paving motif and the diagonal lattice. Although in concept this is a place of privacy, it might be a bit of a struggle finding repose with so much going on.

Scale/Proportion

In considering the quantity of structure in relation to the space it defines, this first garden seems scaled perfectly. The panels and beams are in no way overpowering, nor do they seem weak, and an aura of quietude pervades the scene.

In the second garden, it is not so much the sizes or the quantities of the structural elements as their colors that seem a bit overpowering. The combination of the many brilliant blossoms with the massive furniture does make the space seem choked a bit by a feeling of romanticism. A few less hanging baskets, natural wood colors, perhaps a more sober sculpture, and this too would have offered a pleasant place for privacy.

Style
Again, the first seems all of a piece, with the possible exception of the planted wheelbarrow, which clashes with the ornate Victorian furniture.

Similarly, in the second garden, everything is very romantic, with the exception of the Adirondack furniture, which is too massive and formless for this setting.

Additional Hardscape Functions
Ornamentation certainly makes a case for itself in both of these gardens. Components for *dimensionality* and *outdoor living* are evident as well.

Application
Style aside, this approach of erecting simple lattice panels to create a cozy corner is applicable in most any urban, suburban, or rural backyard.

Planting
6-2: Pelargonium, Petunia, Lobelia, Helichrysum

6-3: Begonia, Hosta, Petunia, Fuchsia

A Quiet Room

Privacy can be achieved simply from creating a sense of being removed, out of the flow of traffic, apart from the goings-on. We can still be visible, not hard to find, yet feel comfortably alone in a quiet place. It takes very little effort to achieve this quality, as the garden in **6-4** demonstrates.

Open lattice frames about halfway down the garden create a division, forming a rear room. Planted in climbing roses, they partially screen off this rear area. At the far end, beneath overhanging trees, we find a paved area with a table and chairs. A private haven—a place to rest or chat in peace and quiet—created by a simple structure strategically placed.

Were a greater degree of privacy desired, several approaches could be employed. The lattice panels could extend further into the yard, creating a smaller opening. These could be placed directly across from one another, as they now are, or staggered, with one extending nearly to the center on one side and the other extending toward the center further down on the opposite side.

Another method for increasing privacy here would be to place the structures further down the lawn, making the rear room smaller. Generally, the more space we feel around us, the more exposed we feel.

Finally, if the planted border on the right side swept out into the lawn at some point, the rear would have been less visible. As it is, however, that rear seating area, well ensconced within a leafy bower, offers a pleasantly private place with no sense of confinement or restriction.

Scale/Proportion

The panels fit beautifully within the space they occupy. Had they been lower, such that they even hinted at the possibility of a view over them, they would have lost their effectiveness. The paved area in the rear is likewise perfectly minimal, bespeaking of intimacy rather than festivity.

6-4 This open area is intentionally oversized to allow for family activities in an outdoor, private setting.

Style

This is an informal, country-style garden. The lattice panels and the stone paving work well, as does the rattan furniture.

Additional Hardscape Functions

Delineation of space is evident, and the various sculpture pieces placed within the beds bring *balance*.

Application

Countless rear properties or backyards—even very small lots—could benefit from this approach.

Planting

Ligustrum ovalifolium 'Argenteum,' Syringa 'Palabin,' Sisyrinchium, Camellias, boxwood topiary, *Rosa 'Felicite Perpetue,'* Espalier apples, Abutilon, myrtle.

Room by a Lake

A more elaborate method for creating privacy is to construct or erect a free-standing garden house—or as it is generally called, a *gazebo* **(6-5)**. Privacy is achieved here not by hiding but by encapsulating. Such a structure need not be enclosed—it can in fact be quite open yet still provide the sense of personal privacy.

Imagine being on the grassy banks of this small lake, on a blanket, say, with a picnic basket. Would you feel a sense of privacy? Probably not very strongly, unless you knew yourself to be the only person within a hundred miles—and even then, you might feel exposed and vulnerable to intrusion. Now place yourself within this gazebo, and you will appreciate instantly the sense of security, of privacy, even this open structure affords.

6-5 An elegant gazebo gives a sense of privacy within an open landscape.

Besides the fact that this structure offers shelter, from rain, for example, simply being in it with the wide-open world around us provides a sense enclosure and makes us feel secure without the least sense of confinement. This is the appeal these structures have. They render a subtle sense of privacy without separating us from the garden. This is no doubt why gazebos have been built into gardens around the world throughout history. When well designed and situated, they offer the best of two worlds, providing a private sanctuary from which to enjoy an open garden.

Scale/Proportion

Comfortably seating four, this structure has a width-to-height ratio that is quite classic, tending to the elegant in its proportions. In addition, it is neither too large nor too small for its environment.

Style

This is a very elegant structure situated at the edge of a fairly natural but well-tended area. It serves to blend the civilized world with the natural world, in that it is representative of the former yet so open to and partaking of the latter. The overall style could be called "rural elegant."

Additional Hardscape Functions

Ornamentation and *dimensionality.*

Application

The decision to include a gazebo in a garden should not be made lightly. Many people have the idea they would like to place one somewhere in their yard, but gazebos are not easy to incorporate without looking very contrived, as they so often do. Generally, they look best with ample space around them, as is found in rural or estate settings. But they can still be used in smaller, suburban gardens, if care is taken to integrate them with their surroundings.

Planting

Daylily, flowering crab apple.

Working with a Gazebo

One approach to making a gazebo work with its environment, besides integrating it with the surroundings, is to make it dominate the surroundings and require the environment to work with it. That would seem to be the approach taken with the garden shown in **6-1** (page 162).

Although this gazebo, in fact, invites attention, it does afford a sense of privacy for its inhabitants. Designed as part of a show garden, it can be used by the whole family and provides a sheltered area for children to play in on wet days.

Such a structure offers an entirely different way of enjoying the garden, as anyone who has lounged around inside one will testify. In Medieval and Renaissance Europe, often such bowers were built in remote corners of grand estates. The lord of the manor and his entourage would journey out there to enjoy the out-of-doors while benefiting from a few amenities and the security of a roof. In England, they liked to take their tea in such quaint corners of their properties, and even we common folk can enjoy summerhouses in similar fashion (though we might lack the great service the grand lords commanded).

> **A FEW THOUGHTS ON**
> **Gardens & Architecture**
>
> Generally, prominent architectural elements in the garden should reflect the architecture of the home. We don't simply appreciate the sense of place this produces, but also enjoy the harmony created between garden and home. Ornamental elements such as planters and large pots, fences, pergolas, and benches all look better and make the garden look better when there is visible harmony with the architecture of the home.

Scale/Proportion
Intentionally oversized—a case of effectively going out of scale.

Style
Tudor.

Additional Hardscape Functions
Stone walls and log fences and the wattle fence around the property give *dimensionality* and *balance*.

Application

In theory, many gardens could support a gazebo, but in practice, this doesn't seem to be the case. I have seen a lot of gazebos that just looked silly, usually because there was no attempt to integrate the structure with the landscape. They seem to work best when ensconced properly in their setting, either through plantings or by being tucked into some sunken area of the garden.

Planting

Willow, Azalea, birch, foxglove, daylily, ivy, hawthorne, Allium, mixed annuals.

Trysting Place

As demonstrated with the last project, a place need not be hidden from the outside to provide a sense of seclusion from within. Making spaces in tree-tops is not often possible, but where it is, the result can be wonderful **(6-6).**

There is no difficulty in locating this arboreal haven, but inside you can feel quite lost to the world. Though solidly built and meant to last, this tree house, with its enclosing foliage and gossamer draping, creates a private and romantic retreat, designed, it would seem, for lovers. There is nothing quite like looking out and seeing birds as your nearest neighbors, and reaching out to touch the leaves

A FEW THOUGHTS ON
Romance

I have not seen it done much, nor have I had the opportunity myself, but it would be quite easy (and wonderful) to create gardens designed specifically for romance: A quiet, almost secret entry to a softly enclosed space opened only to the sky with beautiful blossoms and wonderful fragrances. Soft places to sit and lie. A little stream or pool with colorful fish nearby. Perhaps delicate wind chimes. It could be magical, and the possibilities are endless.

6-6 A romantic bower provides aerial privacy.

in the tops of shrubs and trees. Transporting, it is, and many a tryst has taken place in just such cozy nooks, above the mundane world below.

Scale/Proportion
Although the structure is quite substantial, the enfolding foliage and drapery soften and camouflage it, keeping it perfectly in proportion.

Style
Romantic.

Additional Hardscape Functions
Ornamentation, dimension, balance.

Application
If you have a border or stand of trees affording pleasant views or a space with enough room around it so that you can plant some trees, a charming tree house such as this one can make a wonderful addition.

Planting
Wisteria, Fatsia, calla lilies, crotons, Hedera, ornamental grasses, and others.

City Sanctuary

Y ou live in the city, and you step out of your home and into your garden in the backyard. You look up and all around you are hundreds of windows of other buildings, with strangers somewhere behind them possibly looking down. You feel like a goldfish in a glass bowl. You go back inside. Such is the problem with urban gardens.

Just about everybody in the city wants a garden that seems beautiful. Although this can be easily achieved, how do you make it a place in which you actually want to spend time? That is the issue we address here, and as it happens, there are at least a couple of effective methods, as this and the next garden demonstrate.

As the "before" picture **6-7** indicates, this was an exposed site with access areas around the perimeter and planting space in the middle. It was hard to be here without feeling exposed. In addition to the problem of exposure, as if under a spotlight, there was the issue of how to create a garden that didn't reveal itself all at once, that left something unseen, to be discovered. What was needed was a garden that had a little of its own privacy and gave the visitor privacy as well **(6-8)**.

To achieve this end, a water garden and a planting bed were created just in front of the entry to the garden, guiding visitors to the right. On the extreme right side, a two-tiered raised planter was built, with a ground-level brick planter

6-7 "Before"—the fishbowl effect.

6-8 "After"—the sense of entering a personal sanctuary.

6-9 Wooden planters on the right gave instant height.   **6-10** A private garden in the middle of the city.

placed in front of it. The walk leads between these two juxtaposed planting areas. A crepe myrtle on the right, a lilac tree in the tall box in the corner, and a dogwood on the left create a natural arbor. Now, it is only when we pass through this bower that the garden is revealed **(6-9).**

As we enter the main patio, a sense of soothing privacy takes hold. On the far side, an overgrown privet to the right and a Virginia Magnolia on the left block out views of and from the opposing buildings **(6-10).** In part because of the smallness of the patio and because of the raised planters, the trees screen the surrounding buildings, while allowing sunshine into the center of the patio in the middle of the afternoon.

Scale

The only structural elements involved here for creating privacy are the water garden and the accompanying planting beds, which direct visitors away from the center of the garden, and the raised wooden planters on the extreme right. The primary wooden planter is 6 feet long, 20 inches tall, and 24 inches deep. Out of the near-left corner of that box rises a 5-foot-tall planter that is 20 inches by 24 inches. This contains the sheltering tree. The tall box, tucked into the corner, helps integrate the planters with the surrounding buildings and brings down the longer, lower box so that both seem comfortably in scale.

Style

Natural.

Planting

Magnolia virginicus, Cornus florida, Amelanchier alnifolia, Lagerstroemia, *Kerria japonica, Chamaecyparis obtusa* 'Gracilis,' Iris, *Hydrangea macrophylla, Vinca minor,* Hosta, Ilex, Cryptomeria, *Pieris japonica.*

Two Rooms &
A Summerhouse

Initially, the garden space was exposed completely, as seen in **6-11.** As it was surrounded by four-story brownstones, the mere thought of being out here was intimidating. A garden was needed and privacy in the garden imperative.

Lattice fencing with shrubs and vines around the perimeter would easily take care of ground-level privacy without creating too much of a sense of enclosure. Trees all around the perimeter might solve the overhead issues, but this garden was for someone who loves plants as well as the sun, and trees everywhere would create too much shade. Although the area was limited (approximately 18 feet wide by 30 feet deep), a small summerhouse would offer the desired privacy without taking up too much valuable growing space **(6-12).**

Shown in **6-13** without the vines that now cover it, this cedar-on-brick room is a cool place to escape the beaming rays of the sun and the curious glances of neighbors, while hearing the splashing of the wall fountain just outside. It also serves well as a private-garden dining room or just as a space to have a morning cup of coffee or an evening glass of wine. In addition, it can be a great place for toddlers to play out of the sun.

Scale/Proportion
This structure is as large as possible without encroaching on the remaining space. The height of the summerhouse was determined by the rear wall, being of the same height.

Style
"Arts and crafts" with contemporary and classical touches.

Additional Hardscape Functions
The paving and the arches have an *ornamental* quality, and the raised planters provide *dimensionality*. This garden is also a good example of using structure for *delineating space*.

6-11 "Before"—an exposed garden site.

6-12 "After"—an umbrella and a summerhouse offer different degrees of privacy.

6-13 Vines will soon cover the roof.

6-14 A copper arbor supports roses and Clematis.

6-15 Roses and Clematis richly intertwined.

Application

This sort of structure could occupy nearly any kind of garden, nearly anywhere, except a front garden, where it would not be appropriate.

Planting

Roses, Polygonum, *Hydrangea paniculata*, *Clematis* x, *Prunus subhirtella*, Pieris, *Ilex* sp., *Hydrangea macrophylla*, *Buxus microphylla*, *Pieris japonica*, Hellebore, Liriope, Buddleia, Spirea, *Cotinus coggygria*, mixed perennials **(6-14** and **6-15)**.

Brick & Lattice Garden House

6-16 The brick-and-lattice garden house. Note the colored-glass blocks used in the base walls.

YOU WILL NEED
Brick, glass block, bluestone, stone dust, four-by-four posts and roofing tar, 2-inch-thick cedar lattice panels, lump hammer or brick hammer, brick set chisel, trowel, shovel, mixing pan or mixer

Although not physically taxing, brick construction does require precision and skill. An in-depth explanation of brick construction is beyond the scope of this book; however, here I do show how this garden house and its adjoining patio were built **(6-16)**.

The brick walls are two courses thick with a slight gap between the courses **(6-17)**. The glass blocks are only a bit thicker than a brick, so two of the same color are used adjacent to one another in the walls. This allows for more light to pass through the wall and gives the glass blocks greater translucence.

Note that a space large enough to take the four-by-four posts was left in the columns at the entrance to the garden house **(6-18)**. The posts were tarred with roofing tar up to the point at which they emerge from the stone coping over the brick.

The lattice consists of standard panels with a total thickness of 2 inches and is made of

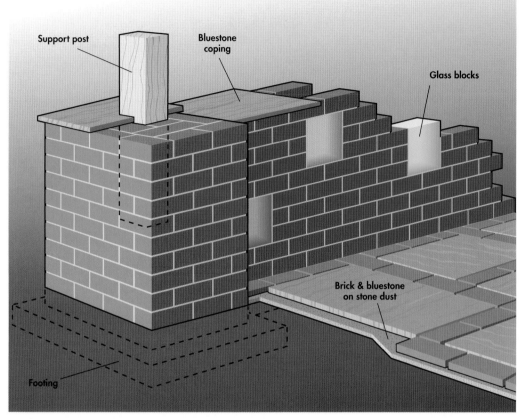

Support post

Bluestone coping

Glass blocks

Brick & bluestone
on stone dust

Footing

6-17 Construction details for the garden house.

6-18 Laying out the patio. The garden house entrance is at the far right—note the spaces left for the posts.

6-19 The entire patio design is determined before the stones and brick are set in the stone dust.

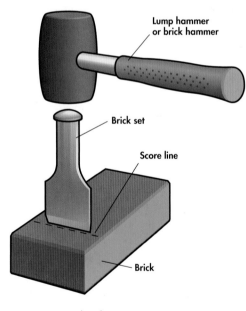

Lump hammer
or brick hammer

Brick set

Score line

Brick

6-20 Using a brick set.

cedar. The arches were custom-made and the lattice panels cut to fit around them.

The patio pattern was laid out first, and only once the entire design was determined were the stones and brick set in stone dust **(6-19)**. The difficulty here was creating a random pattern with different-sized stones, with brick around all four sides of each stone. In many cases, the brick needed to be cut, but as brick is a "soft" material, this can be achieved fairly easily. It can even be cut with a brick hammer; however, for a clean cut, a brick set (chisel) is necessary. Brick can also be cut with a skill saw with an abrasive blade.

To use a brick set, mark the line on the brick where you need to cut **(6-20).** Lay the brick on a bed of sand or stone dust, not on uneven ground. Place the edge of the set or chisel on the line, and hit it sharply with a lump hammer or a brick hammer. Move it along the line across the brick, tapping sharply but not very hard, until it cuts.

Built-In Wall Fountain

6-21 Wall fountain on an existing wall.

Generally, wall fountains are placed on existing walls **(6-21).** The chief difficulty this presents if the basin is a separate component from the fountain is in hiding the plumbing and the electric lines. This is particularly true if access to the back of the wall is not possible or if it is not permissible for lines to be showing in the back. In this case, the only way to effectively hide the works is to go up the middle of the wall **(6-22).** In a brick wall, this will mean removing enough bricks to get a pipe into the wall from the bottom pool to the outflow. It is best if the pipe is large enough to contain the actual tube that will carry the water; such is the case with the electric cord. Using pipe through which the hose and cord can be pulled means that replacing the pump will not require going back into the wall.

Bricks will need to be removed and a pipe inserted through which the electric cord can be pulled. The bricks will need to be cut to a lesser depth before being replaced in the wall. If the wall is not of brick but of some other masonry material, a section can be cut out with an angle grinder and then mortared back over once the lines are in place.

If access to the rear of the wall is possible, then it is simply a matter of drilling two holes

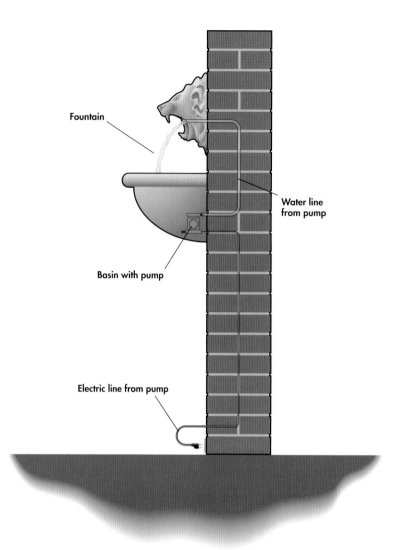

Fountain

Water line
from pump

Basin with pump

Electric line from pump

6-22 The plumbing and electrical works are hidden in the middle of the wall.

for the water line and two for the electric. First, drill the hole where the mask or rosette is to go. Suspend a plumb line from this to mark where the basin is to go, and drill another hole that will be behind the basin. Drop a string through the top hole from the front, down the back of the wall, and pull it through the bottom hole. Tie a string to a tube of the proper size, and pull it up and through the top hole from the back of the wall to the front. Be sure to leave enough to attach to the outflow device (the mask or whatever). The extra can be cut off later once the right length is determined. Drill holes for the electric lines large enough to get the plug through. Drop a string from the top to the bottom, pull it through, tie the plug to the top of the string, and pull it from the bottom.

It is important to place the outflow and the basin near enough to one another so that there is not too much splash. Even a fairly small amount of splash-out will drain the bottom basin and eventually burn out the pump. These fountains that are supplied with pumps normally have a flow adjustment on the pump. To get the proper volume and rate of discharge, simply adjust the outflow on the pump.

CHAPTER 7

Structure for Outdoor Living

In many parts of America, particularly rural America, and many other parts of the world, using the out-of-doors for dining and entertaining just wasn't done. This could be because for people in those regions, a "garden" had always meant either a vegetable garden or a flower garden. Outdoors was where you worked, and indoors where you lived.

The concept of a garden as a space in which to spend time has just begun to be understood in areas remote from cities, with their patios, or the suburbs, with their pools and decks. Along with this greater use of the garden have come all manner of structural elements essential to outdoor living **(7-1 and 7-2)**.

The process often starts by enclosing a lawn with plantings and placing a little paving, thereby creating an outdoor "room" **(7-3).** Soon come other elements: a table and chairs, a pergola for shade, a built-in barbecue for easy cooking, or a gazebo to sit in and listen to the rain. Paths inevitably follow, leading to more rooms with a rock garden, a pool, benches, or a birdbath. All of these structural elements help create and enhance outdoor-living areas. Many of the gardens presented throughout this book contain structures for outdoor living. Here, we look at a few gardens designed specifically for this purpose.

7-1 A simple bench placed in a pleasant spot invites outdoor living.

7-2 A hammock beneath a grape arbor provides a peaceful place to pass some time.

7-3 A small paved area with a comfortable chair may be all that's needed.

Two Rooms &
A Water Garden

Is there some part of your property to which you find yourself gravitating—some little corner in which you would like to spend some time? It is just a matter of installing a few elements to establish an outdoor-living space. You may need only a little paving, with a table and a couple of chairs. Even a hammock strung between a fence post and a tree will bring you out into your garden and provide you with delicious moments beneath the sky.

I don't know how many urban and suburban plots I've seen that looked more or less like the yard shown in **7-4**. I've always been struck by the great potential of these lots, just waiting to be realized. It so happened this owner wanted something very simple that he could use for entertaining and dining.

Had we simply made a large, undifferentiated patio with plantings around the outside, the garden would not have afforded enough privacy or been very inviting. In an urban environment such as this, it is easy to feel exposed without some level of enclosure. Here, the space was enclosed by narrowing the paving and increasing the plantings on either side **(7-5)**. The larger, further area is for entertaining, while the nearer space is for private dining in a garden setting.

7-4 "Before"—an open space awaiting a garden.

7-5 "After"—a garden divided into two areas.

7-6 Private dining and room for larger-scale entertaining created simply by altering the paving and the planting.

7-7 The water feature serves as an ornament and a focal point, central along the long axis.

To the far end is a water garden, with the sound of the water splashing, which adds to the pleasure of being out here. The raised water feature also serves as a focal point throughout the garden.

Scale/Proportion

Here, we will look at the relationship of the expanse of paving to the planting and the relationship of the two paved areas to each other and the water feature **(7-6)**. There might have been a little less paving overall and a little more planting had there been no need to be able to accommodate ten or more people on occasion. The garden is shown only a year after having been planted, so the amount of foliage will increase over time. The water feature, with the planter behind it, is large enough to draw the eye toward it and invite investigation without overly dominating that end of the patio **(7-7)**. The two areas are distinct enough in size to enhance the impression of two rooms. The near area could have been a little larger without destroying this impression and would have felt a little more inviting. As it is, there is a greater sense of privacy in the small garden and more expansiveness to the larger area.

Style

Casual and informal, with (except for the Oriental pots) a slight European touch to the arrangement and the type of fountain.

Additional Hardscape Functions

We experience *delineation of space* from narrowing the paving, and the water feature serves as a *focal point*. A few elements of *ornamentation,* such as the two masks, add interest.

Application

This is a very simple design and could be used nearly anywhere. It is simply a paved area made to feel like two separate rooms by narrowing the paving and bringing in the plants. The water feature and ornaments embellish the overall scene.

Planting

Behind the fountain is a threadleaf Japanese maple (*Acer palmatum dissectum*). To either side are Leland cypress and, in a pot, *Physocarpus opulifolius.* Scattered about are crepe myrtle, Sambucus, Cotinus, *Rhododendron* sp., *Euonymus* sp., *Anemone japonica, Hydrangea petiolaris,* Coreopsis, and other perennials. A Cornus hybrid is near the table.

A Quiet Corner

If you have more than a small yard—a suburban backyard, say, or a good-sized rural property—it can be quite delightful to find an inviting little nook and make an outdoor living room out of it. It doesn't take much to make such a place, and once this is done, it becomes a destination. A place to wander back to for a little private contemplation or a quiet chat.

The garden in **7-8** is a bit more than paving and furniture, but not much more. The site was selected for its general pleasantness. A nearby dam spills water over a fall, enlivening the air; tall birches and maples provide dappled shade; and a little level area invites repose.

To enhance these attributes, a retaining wall was built into the bank, rendering a little more level space, which was paved in natural stone. A simple European-style water garden was built, and a weather-resistant table and chairs added, creating a simple, charming place for outdoor pleasures.

A FEW THOUGHTS ON
Building with Berms

One simple method of adding dimensionality to a flat garden site without bringing in boulders and such is to create berms. These mounds of soil can be made several feet tall, and their heights and widths varied for dramatic effect. They can be formed into most any shape and once planted will retain their character essentially forever with little maintenance. They provide instant and inexpensive dimension, allow for additional planting areas, and can dramatically transform a garden.

Scale/Proportion

The designer must have realized it was important not to dominate or in any way compromise the natural, pastoral feeling of this setting. The paved area with its raised fountain is perfectly adequate for accommodating a few people. At the same time, these hard elements are balanced by and take second place to nature **(7-9)**. Note too that the paving is randomly, almost casually, laid with wide grassy joints. The water garden is fairly prominent but suitably simple, easily balanced by the abundant native shrubs and trees. It contributes to the welcoming, civilized feeling, while providing the delicious sounds and sights of splashing water, making this spot a pleasant refuge on warm summer days.

7-8 A remote corner of the property made habitable.

7-9 Paving plus a table and chairs is all it takes to make a place for outdoor living.

7-10 Add a water garden for delightful sounds and sights.

Style

This garden has an Old European feel with Victorian flourishes **(7-10)**. The stone of the paving and the water garden is a local marble—contributing an indigenous element. The setting is relaxed, though the central water feature adds a decidedly classical touch. However, because this garden is situated within woods, it is pervaded by a rustic quality.

Additional Hardscape Functions

There is a slight *ornamental* quality, and the hard elements provide *dimensionality* and *balance*.

Application

It is easy to think this style requires a rustic, woodsy, and spacious setting, but this is not so. The basic idea is to define a fairly remote area—some cozy, inviting corner, for example—in which to spend some time. Paving and minimal furnishings can do this. If you add a little water feature and a lantern or candles, outdoor living can become an enjoyable option in your life.

Planting

Native plants, with paper bark birch (*Betula papyrifera*) and juniper. *Cyperus alternifolius* is in the water.

Outdoor Rooms with Wonderful Views

One reason for creating an outdoor living area is to provide a pleasant place from which to enjoy the surrounding garden or the distant landscape **(7-11)**. Many properties are endowed with some portion offering better views. People often add some form of structure there, creating a destination point and a way to use and enjoy the space.

This hillside property overlooking the Mediterranean Sea had magnificent potential, but that potential had to be developed **(7-12)**. And it was. Just in front of the very private house, the hill was terraced, a level area was created, and a patio was built, where furnishings were placed **(7-13)**. From here, you can enjoy exceptional views of the surrounding garden and the distant scenery. Similar views are

7-11 A patio provides a place to enjoy the garden and the landscape beyond. The Mediterranean Sea is in the distance.

7-12 A Wisteria spills its petals onto the lawn.

available from the house too, but out here you are in the garden, a part of it, and able to fully imbibe the exquisite beauty all around. Convenient to the house, this patio is a great place to come for an evening cocktail or a morning cup of coffee. A table can be quickly set up and unforgettable meals enjoyed in the cool evening air.

Scale/Proportion

There is a pleasant amplitude to the patio—being slightly oversized, it works well in the verdant surroundings. It could have been a little smaller and still worked, but the size it is seems appropriate and is appreciated.

Style

Informal Italian, in that this is a garden room linked closely to the home, but it could also be called "French Mediterranean" or simply "Riviera style."

Additional Hardscape Functions

One thing to notice about this patio is what a pleasant contrast it is to the surrounding greenery, both in color and texture, so in this sense it serves the function of *balance*. Of course, it displays *ornamental* qualities as well.

7-13 Embedded in the garden, the patio affords pleasant views and fragrant scents.

Application

Again, there is no grand scheme here—only the intent to carve out a special place and make it habitable and usable. Any suburban, rural, or estate garden could contain such an area for outdoor living. Even urban lots could contain essentially the same elements, if on a lesser scale.

Planting

Bird-of-paradise, calla lily, foxglove, Calceolaria, Lobelia, Calendula, Mertensia, Myosotis, Phlox, Nemesia, Allysum, *Melaleuca dessicata*, Wisteria, roses.

Garden Patio

Of the many pleasant attributes a garden can possess, an inviting place right off the house in which to sit, read, dine, or entertain is chief among them. It should be a fairly private place, yet not feel confined. It should be accessible, comfortable so that you want to spend some time there, attractive, and unique—reflecting your personal tastes and lifestyle.

We first visited this property in Chapter 2 on dimensionality (see **2-28** and **2-30**). This is the area the brick walk leads to, as you wind your way up through the garden. As the "before" image **7-14** shows, this area was partially enclosed, providing pleasant privacy, with the old olive tree casting dappled shade. But the space had not been developed in any manner to make it useable and enjoyable.

The design called for a brick patio inset with stone here and there, in harmony with the street-side garden **(7-15).** Both the main entrance and the dining room open onto this area, making it convenient for dining and outdoor entertaining and receiving the spillover of indoor-party guests.

The circular design around the olive tree determined the shape of the planting beds—formed at the points of intersection where the walkways meet the main patio **(7-16).** These beds are on all sides of the patio so that we feel ourselves to be thoroughly in the garden while out there. They also soften the space and afford pleasant views in all directions **(7-17** and **7-18).**

In a garden where there is enough space, it is always a treat to have access from the main living area to some other part of the garden **(7-19).** It is an invitation to explore and discover what lies beyond. Here, a path at the far side leads to the rear garden, with a seating area that is sunlit in the morning **(7-20).**

Scale/Proportion

Scale here refers to the relationship of the hardscape to the softscape. The patio needed to be large enough for entertaining and as such is a little out of scale with the surrounding planting beds. The addition of the pots and the hanging baskets, however, ameliorates this.

7-14 "Before"—the space was available, but nothing had yet been done to allow for outdoor living.

7-15 The same scene as the "before" picture after paving and planting had been added.

7-16 Plantings in the center help soften the hardscape.

7-17
Planting areas surround the patio.

7-18 A path leads off the patio to a remote seating area.

7-19 Looking from out in the patio toward the house.

7-20 This corner catches the morning sun. A mosaic makes the space more inviting.

Style

You might call this "California casual" with undercurrents of formality, but I think of it as "arts and crafts." The bricks are laid on sand with an occasional stone worked in, but in a repeating pattern, which lends a touch of formality. The steps are built of brick and stone and are meant to echo the street-side garden walls. Where the walks from the two entries and the gate beneath the arbor intersect, the stones and bricks have been cut to form a seamless interweaving of the three directions with one another and with the circular patio.

There is an Art Nouveau quality to the mosaic seating area, but that too falls within the domain of "arts and crafts."

Additional Hardscape Functions

Delineation of space, ornamentation, and *motion* are all evident here.

Application

Nearly every house has a space close by that could host outdoor living—whether it is a patio, a deck, or some other structure that invites and accommodates use.

Planting

Bougainvillea mantles the doorway, with *Nandina domestica* propping up the opposite side. For substance are Photinia, Camellia, and Azalea. Scattered about are Agapanthus, roses, Iberis, and violets, and in pots are Fuschia, geraniums, Clivia, Shasta daisies, and Begonias.

Three Patios
Interlaced with a Pool

One of the advantages of large properties is that they can be divided into separate settings offering a variety of expressions and experiences. Occasionally, it is preferable to leave large properties large in order to afford expansive views and grand scenes. But more often than not, we can gain considerably more enjoyment from a large property by dividing it into several usable areas. Of course, if the property is ample enough, we can have both.

We saw the entrance to this property in Chapter 3 on instilling motion (in the section on pages 80 to 83, "An Elegant *S*") and the front of the property in Chapter 4 on delineation of space (in the section on pages 128 to 131, "Reflecting Pools with a View"). There, the expansive views were left intact, while a formal terrace was built from which to enjoy them. This is the area behind the house off an enclosed veranda, and as the "before" image **7-21** shows, there was a great deal of space here but no spectacular views.

Two of the design mandates for this space were to offer outdoor living with easy access from the house and to provide for the occasional large celebration with lots of guests. It also needed to be able to accommodate a very large gas grill. Rather than make one big patio, I chose instead to create three smaller interconnecting areas, with water flowing past and lapping the edges of each **(7-22)**. An ample patio near the house connects to a more private dining area that contains the cooking unit, and this area connects to an intermediately sized patio. Together, this series of interconnected rooms can accommodate quite a number of guests. Yet the smaller dining area and the more private third patio lend themselves to a feeling of intimacy.

Creating three interconnected rooms brings forth a sense of motion and discovery as we move from one room to another. This effect will increase as the plants mature. The two Japanese maples, for example, will form a natural arbor between the first and second rooms, creating a pleasant tension as we pass

7-21 "Before"—an open space with lots of potential.

7-22 "After"—three patios interlaced with a koi pool.

7-23 The two Japanese maples will form a natural arbor.

7-24 As the island plantings grow, the third patio will be obscured, creating privacy for that area.

7-25 The water is one contiguous body.

7-26 "Before"—the area of the third patio.

7-27 "After"—the "floating step" connects to the third patio.

through it to the different areas **(7-23)**. Similarly, the *Hydrangea paniculata,* the Buddlea, and the dwarf white pine between the first and third rooms will add to the mystery as they grow to maturity **(7-24)**. While separated by plants, the three spaces are at the same time connected to one another by the contiguous body of water circulating between them. This also adds to the excitement and enjoyment, particularly as we watch the fish swim alongside the patios **(7-25)**, gliding fluidly from one to the next.

The third patio occupies what was previously only an open space at the base of an old weeping beach tree (*Fagus sylvatica 'Pendula'*) **(7-26)**. I might have made this a garden to be enjoyed from the two paved areas or perhaps a lawn bordered by gardens, had it not been for the mandate to have ample entertaining space. But I also felt it would be a lot of fun to have this somewhat removed area to go to, where a table or lounge chairs can be placed—a quiet spot where one can soak up the sun.

To accentuate the separateness of this area and to create one contiguous body of water, I designed a floating step between the two patios **(7-27)**. Of course, it isn't really floating. The bluestone paving is cantilevered over a concrete pillar, allowing the fish to glide by at our feet. This too adds a gentle excitement to the setting.

> ## A FEW THOUGHTS ON
> ### Gardens & Fun
>
> I don't hear it mentioned much, but one of the driving intents in almost all my garden designs is the element of *fun.* I feel that gardens should be fun, as sailing sticks down streams as a child was fun, as growing your favorite alpines over beautiful stones is fun, as water gardens are fun. Often gardens seem to be designed with *concept* as the driving force, and those gardens are often spectacular or dramatic, but not particularly fun. Most of us prefer a garden in which it feels good to be alive!

7-28 The water garden can support more than a hundred fish of various species.

Although construction of these pools is the same as for a concrete swimming pool, the intent was to create a natural habitat for aquatic flora and fauna **(7-28).** To contribute to the effect, the plaster was dyed gray—not so dark as to obscure the fish but dark enough to make the interior construction disappear **(7-29** and **7-30).**

Scale/Proportion

The three patios taken together comprise quite a lot of hardscape and might for some people be too much. Yet within the context of the surrounding garden environment, they seem well scaled to me, especially with the abundant planting all around, as seen earlier in **7-22.**

Style

A contemporary design infused with a sense of the natural.

7-29 The cement of the pool interior was dyed gray to give the water a more natural look.

7-30 Vertical accents balance against the horizontal surfaces.

Additional Hardscape Functions

Delineation of space is evident. There is definitely a sensation of *motion* as we look at or move among the three areas. The rear patio has the quality of *privacy*.

Application

This sort of layout requires considerable space, not only to hold the three patios (you might have space for the actual structures); rather, the patios should also have considerable open space or softscape around them to be in balance.

Planting

Here, we find Japanese maples, *Hydrangea paniculata*, Buddlea, dwarf white pine, various ornamental grasses, *Prunus* x *cistena*, birch, Iris, and *Cornus kousa*. In the water are water lilies (*Nymphaea* x), pickerel rush (*Pontederia cordata*), red-stemmed Sagittaria (*Sagittaria lancifolia 'Ruminoides'*), umbrella palm (*Cyperus alternifolius*), and water hyacinth (*Eichhornia crassipes*).

Poured-Concrete Retaining Wall & Footing

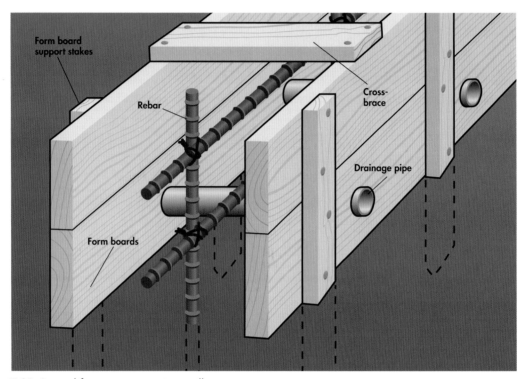

7-31 Poured footing or retaining wall.

Brick, concrete mortar, sand, aggregate, rebar and wire (as needed), rubber mallet, stone hammer, wood for form(s), PVC pipe, trowel, shovel, mixing pan or mixer

When planning to pour a footing or a retaining wall, you will need to consider the climate of the region. The setup shown in **7-31** can be used for creating a footing or poured-concrete wall in temperate climates. In areas of frost, this setup would be used for the footing, and the form boards could be extended upward with more rebar, to create the footing and the wall in one single, monolithic pour. If there is to be a tall wall, a footing would first be poured in the same manner, but wider than the wall, such that when the wall is built on top, approximately 6 inches of footing would extend out past both edges of the wall. Another form can then be built on this footing and the wall poured, once the footing has cured **(7-32).**

The horizontal runs of rebar should be approximately 6 inches apart, from side to side and top to bottom. Thus, the wider the footing

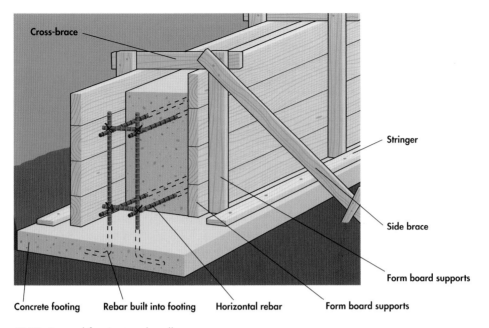

Cross-brace

Stringer

Side brace

Form board supports

Form board supports

Concrete footing   Rebar built into footing   Horizontal rebar

7-32 Poured footing and wall.

or the taller the wall, the more horizontal pieces of rebar are used. The vertical pieces of rebar help to hold the horizontal ones in place and add strength. These can either be anchored in the footing, if the footing is a separate pour, or simply driven into the ground, if in a temperate climate or below the frost line. Not shown in either illustration are the end boards.

Pressure-treated two-by material (2 x 6 or 2 x 12, for example) is excellent for creating strong forms. These are braced with stakes driven into the ground and screwed to the boards. Cross braces add more support and prevent the boards from bowing outward under the pressure of the concrete.

The rebar is positioned properly and wired together to the vertical rebar. The inside of the forms can be oiled for easy removal. If pouring a footing, the drainpipes are not included, but for a retaining wall, they are. PVC is an excellent material for this purpose and can either be left in the wall or, as the concrete is setting up, twisted every now and again, to prevent them from binding to the concrete, and removed when the concrete has set. If the pipes are left in the wall, they can be cut flush with the wall once the forms have been removed.

If pouring a footing first, it will be necessary to attach a stringer to help hold the supports. This can be attached to the footing before it sets up or screwed on with masonry screws after. If it is to be below-grade, there is no harm in attaching it to the wet cement with anchor bolts and leaving it on after the forms are dismantled. Note that the footing should be a minimum of 6 inches in depth or below the frost line for a low (2- to 3-foot) retaining wall.

The concrete mix you use will depend on the look you want. For example, if you want an exposed aggregate look, you will need to select the aggregate—small, washed stone, for example, or a rough gravel. This will be mixed with sand and cement, and the proportions will depend on the particular aggregate, but generally a mix of one-part cement, three-parts sand, and five-parts gravel works well. Ask your supplier for the recommended mix according to the aggregate you choose. The stone aggregate gives a great deal of strength to the wall, but if you want a smooth wall with no stone showing, you will need to apply a plaster coat once it has been built. This is simply a thin coat of one part masonry cement to two or three parts sand, troweled on.

Raised Mortared Brick
or Block Fountain

A typical application of a poured footing
would be for the base of a water garden or a
raised formal fountain **(7-33).** The retaining
walls might also be poured or laid in brick.

Once the pool is marked out on the ground,
excavate to below frost line. If the base of the
water garden is above the frost line, freezing
could heave the foundation and generate
cracks and leaks.

Pour the footing for the walls and floor
of the fountain from approximately three parts
sand, one part Portland cement and two part
gravel. It's fine to throw small stones and
rubble into the footing as well. In very cold
areas reinforce the concrete with rebar.
(See Chapter 7, "Poured-Concrete Retaining
Wall"). Let the footing and floor cure a day
or two before building up the foundation to
just below grade with block. The concrete will
turn from greenish to gray when it has cured
sufficiently to lay on new mortar. It is also a
good idea to apply a coating of Weld-Crete
or some similar agent for binding fresh (wet)
concrete to newly hardened concrete. Once
this has dried, the block walls for the
foundation can be built up.

Alternatively, rather than pour a footing and
then build a foundation of block on top of that,
the footing can be poured as one piece from
below the frost line to just below grade with no
block employed. In this case, allow an extra

day or two for the footing/foundation to dry.
Once that is achieved, the brick walls for the
fountain can be built. For this, follow standard
brick masonry techniques, the primary
concerns with brick being to lay every brick
straight, perfectly in line with the one beneath it
and perfectly level front to back and side to
side. You will also want the joints between the
bricks and between the rows to be consistent
throughout.

The pump will have an electric line running
from it to outside the pool and a tube which
carries the water to where the water enters the
pool, usually via an ornament of some kind.
Both the electric cord and the tube will need to
be run through piping so that the pump can be
removed for cleaning or replacing without
breaking into the walls of the masonry.

One method of building in the plumbing is
to build the pipe into the walls during
construction and then seal around them with a
watertight caulking. Another method is to build
the basin completely, apply the watertight coat,
then build in the plumbing up the sides of the
walls and plaster over them so that no
plumbing is seen. Either way works if done
properly. Do realize that the PVC pipe that runs
from the basin up the side of the pool or
through the middle of it will carry water as high
as the level in the basin when filled, so be sure
to run it higher than water level and if in a cold
climate, use thick wall, (schedule 40 or
schedule 80) PVC or another material which
will not crack in freezing temperatures. Make
sure the plug from the electric cord can fit
easily through the pipe.

Another, foolproof waterproofing agent if
directions are followed is a combination of
materials sold as Mulasticoat. A twenty-pound

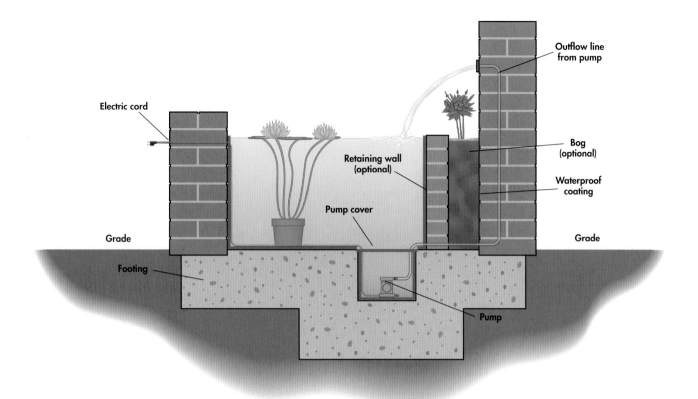

7-33 Raised formal fountain.

bag of a "scratch coat" material is mixed with forty-eight ounces of water into a pancake batter consistency, and this is rolled or brushed onto a clean, dry masonry surface and let to dry for two days. The liquid Mulasticoat is stirred and applied with a roller. When it turns from power blue to dark blue (at least two hours and not more than three days later), a second coat is applied. After two days the pool can be filled with water. Sources for this can be found on the Internet.

Once built, the basin's walls and floor need to be made water retentive. The watertight coating that is used is critical. Cement is not in and of itself waterproof. Special mixtures must be used to ensure water retention. The simplest, and that used by swimming-pool makers is to mix "waterproof" cement with marble dust— available at many masonry supply yards. The

proportions are given on the bag. This creates a very plastic plaster which when troweled on gives a smooth, waterproof surface. At least two coats are recommended.

Once the interior of the pool is entirely waterproof, it is possible to build a retaining wall inside the pool to create a planting area, should this be desired. Filled with soil, this will become a bog from the moisture seeping through the retaining wall, or alternately, it is possible to give this wall a watertight coat and have an ordinary planting bed. This permits plants to grow behind the fall of water and can be quite attractive.

This sort of water feature can be very complex. It can have a drain with a gate valve, one or more fountains or inlet devices; it can have a float valve allowing the pool to automatically top off when the water level falls;

and it can be cleaned by a skimmer leading to an external pump.

Alternatively, the raised fountain can be simple. Rather than waterproofing the interior, a liner can be used over the masonry, held in place by the coping. Rather than running a pipe for the water through the masonry, the fountain can rise directly out of a pump fitted with a pre-filter or mechanical filter. In this instance, we need only concern ourselves with running the electric cord discreetly out of the fountain.

Keep in mind when building a formal fountain that if the walls of the basin are of a cementitious material, it will need to be filled and drained several times, over a few weeks to leach out the lime and generate a stable pH necessary for healthy fish. It can also be given a diluted muriatic acid wash to quicken the process, but this does to some extent weaken the cement. Alternatively, a sealant can be brushed over the finished surface to seal the lime in.

CHAPTER 8

Structure for Ornamentation

Ornament is nearly as important to a garden as it is to a home. "Nearly," because a garden is a type of ornament in and of itself, particularly when it possesses an abundance of beautiful plants **(8-1)**. A home is a necessity that we choose to ornament and thereby elevate. We bring decoration and art to a home, through its design, in the furnishings, and through the various objects with which we choose to surround ourselves in order to experience beauty. We create gardens for their innate, ornamental value—for their beauty. We then can bring additional ornamentation to them, to give a home to a favorite object, to highlight some corner, to embellish, enliven, to bring more depth—to make them more beautiful **(8-2)**.

How much and what sort of ornament will always be a matter of taste and, of course, should be influenced by the style of the garden. But unless we are dealing with a strictly formal arrangement, there is a lot of leeway in how we dress up our gardens; what to one person is art might to another be overdone **(8-3, 8-4)**. With that said, there are some general parameters and principles that can help us determine what works and what doesn't.

Here, we look at a few very different kinds of gardens—some having only a few ornamental elements and others that are almost entirely composed of ornaments. Presented first are ornamental portions of gardens. These are followed by gardens that display ornaments throughout. We finish with two gardens that are almost entirely ornaments in and of themselves.

8-1 The garden itself is an ornament.

8-3 Ornamental objects can both harmonize and contrast effectively with plants.

8-2 An ornamental entrance welcomes you into the garden.

8-4 A beautifully inlaid bench adds elegance to a garden walk.

Order As Ornament

The next three gardens demonstrate different ways of bringing ornamentation to a portion of a garden through the attractive arrangement of various plants, and are discussed here under one heading. "Scale/Proportion," "Style," "Additional Hardscape Functions," and "Planting" are not applicable and so have been omitted.

It is interesting how closely connected order is to ornamentation as well as art is—how, in fact, order is a precursor to ornamentation and ornamentation to art. In these next three gardens, all that's been done is that the plants have been given order, yet the result is highly ornamental.

The potting shed is usually the messiest portion of a garden. Yet in **8-5,** it is a place of charm, owing primarily to the neat arrangement of the pots. On the left, pots all of a type are suspended in wire loops equally spaced. Next to that are fairly uniform pots all in rows neatly set on a series of shelves. Beneath, similar pots are set out on a table, and to the right is a somewhat more eclectic grouping, whose color contrasts make them look especially pretty.

All this may be quite obvious and perhaps not very noteworthy; however, there is an important lesson here that has to do with the effectiveness and ornamental value of good order, also evident in the garden in **8-6.** This is nothing more than various succulents planted in square and round pots placed alternately all in rows. The placement creates a design—a pattern—which is the basis of decorative art.

The garden in **8-7** takes the notion of order one step further through the use of the more elaborate structure of the arch. Actually, this is a series of arches united into a single structure, along which Laburnum and Wisteria have been trained. This still involves simply the ordering and arrangement of plants, but the result is more than a pattern—it is the emergence of pattern into a third dimension. What we have here is a harmony of graceful lines repeated through space in the creation of a scene through which we are invited to pass.

8-5 Ordering of potted plants can bring ornamentation to a corner of the garden.

8-6 Sedum in square and round pots, organized in an attractive display.

8-7 Training Laburnum over metal arches creates a charming setting.

Application

The fastest avenue to ornamentation is through orderly arrangement to the point of creating patterns. Pots neatly arranged around a patio provide ornamentation as do plants forced to follow the lines of some structure. In fact, patterns created out of many sorts of elements can bring forth the quality of ornamentation and can be applied anywhere and everywhere in all kinds of gardens.

Country Elegance
Everywhere

Large properties can be made up of various small gardens, each different from the other. In such cases, ornaments can be used to enhance the differences or, contrarily, to help unite them (8-8). If a similar style of ornament is used in the various areas, a quality of *unity through variety* can be achieved. If very different styles of ornament are employed, the differences of each space will be enhanced, accentuating the experience of *variety*. Either approach can be effective and attractive.

We visited the property in 8-9 earlier in Chapters 1 and 5, on balance and focal points, respectively. Here, we look at several of the different gardens the property possesses. In each area, we find a similar quality and style of ornamentation. This gives the entire property a sense of unity despite the different treatments of the spaces.

The formal perennial garden is an ornament in itself, by virtue of its design. It is also ornamented generously with the lattice fence, the vine towers, the paths, the pots, and the birdbaths. We see again in the path that leads from this symmetrical layout to the front of the house, ornamentation through the powerful device of *order into pattern* (8-10).

It is made of slate laid in a random ashlar pattern. Framed on one side by a flower border and on the other by a stone wall with finial-topped columns, this path has the same quality and style of ornamentation as found in the formal garden. The walk leads past the front entry to the side garden, where we find the vegetable garden. Even here, a quality of formal ornamentation serves to elevate the scene and connect it to everything else (8-11). The walkway pattern here changes to a diamond design of slate in a gravel bed. The plain picket fence around the vegetable garden is highlighted by formal capped columns, and inside the vegetable garden is a formally designed bench flanked by raised urn planters (8-12).

8-8 Vine towers, lattice fencing, and the birdbath add ornamental touches.

8-9 The formal arrangement is in itself ornament.

8-10 Local slate makes a pretty walkway.

8-11 Slate laid in diamond patterns in a gravel bed makes a pleasant path.

8-12 Even the vegetable garden contains an ornamental bench of the same style of other ornaments throughout the garden.

This diamond-design walk meets another ashlar pattern, leading in one direction to a rock garden and in the other to the ornate pergola seen on page 146 in Chapter 5 on focal points (8-13). The rock garden (8-14) has been framed in the same slate, elevating it into an almost formal composition, despite the natural placement of the stones and the drifts of plants.

To the side of the elaborate pergola (8-15) is a perennial garden. Here, too, there is a similar quality of elegant ornamentation in the central stone urn and the deftly woven wattle fence. Across the gravel walk stands a row of hypertufa alpine planters. Throughout this garden then, from one garden space to another, we find a similar quality and style of ornamentation that creates a *unification of place* within a variety of garden settings (8-16).

Scale/Proportion

The only area in which anything might seem out of scale is the front entry, where the finials look a little large for the columns (or the columns too small for the finials), but the owner did this to clearly mark the entrance and to establish at the entry the formality found in the home. As for the rest—the widths of the walks, the quantity of the ornaments, and their dimensions—all seem very well proportioned.

8-13 Everywhere detail and decoration greet the eye.

8-14 The rock garden is framed in the same slate used for the walkways.

8-15 Ornamental details add to this pergola.

Style
Country formal.

Additional Hardscape Functions
There are several *focal points* throughout the garden. Various structures provide *balance* and add *dimensionality*.

Application
Ornamentation was used here to unify divergent garden rooms by repeating not specific elements but the same quality and style of elements. This principle can be applied to any garden consisting of several different spaces.

Planting
The formal garden: *Geranium* x 'Johnson's Blue,' *Geranium sanguineum,* peonies, Siberian Iris, Japanese Iris, Hemerocallis, Astilbe, Delphinium, *Silphium perfoliatum,* and others

Along the diamond-slate path: *Cerastium tomentosum, Sedum acre,* and evening primrose

The rock garden: Dianthus, *Sedum acre,* and *Hemerocallis* x

8-16 From one end to the other, this garden is unified by a single style of ornamentation.

A Sculpture Garden

Some prefer to use ornamentation very sparingly, with an object here or there, or with perhaps one area of the garden made to look ornamental **(8-17)**. Others enjoy using ornament abundantly throughout the garden. The garden in **8-18** is of the latter category. This garden belongs to devoted plants-people, who are also collectors of unusual art, which they enjoy incorporating into their garden.

A sea of foliage and a sprinkling of blossoms, punctuated by bold forms in metal and stone, characterize this upstate New York garden **(8-19** and **8-20)**. Everywhere you look some ornamental object rises up from an eclectic display of species such that these *objets d'art* are as much a part of the garden as are the plants.

Mostly historic in nature and collected from a wide range of locales over a number of years, these ornaments have special significance to the owners of this garden. They love coming across them as they work in their garden and picking them out of the undulant foliage as they sit on the veranda and look out over the landscape. This, of course, is one of the primary reasons for ornamenting a garden—to display your favorite objects in an outdoor setting **(8-21)**.

Although not to everyone's taste, these various farm implements, finials, stones, and sculptures also give character, balance, and solidity to the landscape **(8-22)**. Repetition of form—seen in the spires, spheres, arches, and stony plinths—helps bring unity to an otherwise loosely structured landscape. There are a great many species combined in this garden, and so the hardscape elements work quite well in integrating the total landscape.

Scale/Proportion

Here, no object or combination of objects dominates its given sphere of influence. There is so much varied foliage that the hardscape elements seem on the whole well suited to their surroundings.

8-17 A mere well-placed stone brings ornamentation to a garden.

8-18 Everywhere we look ornaments rise up out of the eclectic planting.

8-19 Collected over the years, these objects hold special meaning for the owners.

8-20 The *objets d'art* are as much a part of the garden as are the plants.

8-21 A unique garden with equal importance placed on the plants and the ornaments.

8-22 Repetition of form helps bring an element of unity.

Style

"Unique," I think, would characterize this style. It would be contemporary but for the abundance of unpruned species that give the garden a natural look—natural except for the many unusual objects found throughout.

Additional Hardscape Functions

Balance and *dimensionality* are additional functions of these ornaments.

Application

This is a garden created by people who love plants and architectural ornaments equally and who like to see them in combination. This can be done anywhere, in any style of garden, depending on the particular objects selected. For example, a formal landscape would obviously require an entirely different selection of objects, but the principle is applicable anywhere.

Planting

Weeping white pine (*Pinus strobus 'Pendula'*), Serbian spruce (*Picea omorika*), Japanese umbrella pine (*Sciadopitys verticillata*), *Abies* sp., miniature goats beard, *Tsuga* sp., *Fagus sylvatica 'Tortuosa,' Fagus sylvatica 'Tortuosa Purpurea,'* Chinese elms, Coreopsis, Montauk daisies, *Phlox stolonifera*, juniper, Potentilla, Iris, Hosta, Coreopsis, lilies, Rhododendron, and Chamaecyparis.

Ornamentally Unique

Once we begin to realize that we are not obliged to make our gardens look like the gardens of other people—that they can have all manner of elements we may never have seen before and still be a garden, still be beautiful—we can open the doors to our imagination and invite our creative potential out to play **(8-23).**

Apparently, the owner/designer of this garden never got the memo about what a suburban garden was supposed to be like. No dominating lawn, no specimen tree, no foundation planting clipped into geometric forms—nothing to let you know you're in a neighborhood just like hundreds of thousands of other neighborhoods across the country. Instead, she has used unique sculptures, original fencing, dynamic plantings, and one-of-a-kind water gardens **(8-24).** What a relief.

The front entry is an iron arbor with opaque panels to either side flanked by dramatic plantings and bold contrasts. Perfectly framed in the background is an iron-and-glass water feature. "Welcome to my world" the place seems to say. To the left, after entering, is the primary outdoor-living area of the front yard **(8-25).** How many homes in suburbia have claimed the front yard for such personal, private use? How many suburban front yards get any use at all?

An unusual combination of materials and forms combine into a richly textured garden, which is both a treat to see and a pleasure in which to be. Both the planting and the hardscape elements are bold in form, yet there is a delicacy to the scene, probably due to the masterful use of detail. This is apparent not only in the grasslike leaves growing out of the grill, the feathery grass inflorescence, and the spikelike sculpture embedded in a foliar mimicry, but also in the perforations of the chair, the details in the fur of the cast-stone wolfhound, and the vivid colors with their strong contrasts and smooth harmonies. The setting is one of brilliant detail and well-thought-out juxtapositions.

8-23 An unusual entry to a suburban front yard.

8-24 A pierced-iron wall with a water feature.

8-25 A richly textured combination of materials and forms replaces the usual lawn.

8-27
Structures
and plants
are wed
through forms
and colors.

8-26 Iron water towers with curved cuts filled with pebbles imitate the calla lilies in the background.

The rear of the property is equally unique. From the paving upward, we are struck by bold contrasts of form and texture between elements in proximity within broader harmonies uniting one area with another. Quite an excellent method, it would seem, for maximizing variety without creating chaos.

Everything here is of ornamental value—the intention seeming to be to re-create natural forms in man-made materials and harmonize them with the plantings. Note, for example, the resemblance between the cut-iron water towers filled with pebbles and the unfurling leaves of the red calla lilies in the background **(8-26)** and the gracefully plantlike iron sculpture in the border with the purple pot and blue glass balls. Nature and art are married in a seamless union of harmonies and contrasts, even down to the finest details **(8-27)**. The mosaic, the glass balls, the iron sculpture, and the blue pot mimic the foliar colors, while the balls, pot, and sculpture repeat the plant forms. Notice, for example, the shape of the pot and that of the Bergenia leaves at its base and the lines of the sculpture with the grasses behind it.

8-28 A whimsical flourish in melding man-made forms with plants.

At the extreme rear of the property, we find the same principles applied, with a more capricious flourish. Man-made inflorescence emerges from bold tufts of ornamental grasses (*Miscanthus sinensis*), which provide screening to the dunking pool. Iron sculptures and repeating colors add to the ornamentation **(8-28).**

Scale/Proportion

There are many ornamental objects throughout this garden. This could easily be distracting and overwhelming, had it not been for the abundance of plants and particularly the skillful blending and uniting of these objects with the plants through color mimicry and form repetition. As it is, the larger elements are situated in the more open areas, and the smaller objects are placed within discrete planting beds where they balance well with the flora.

Style

This is a contemporary garden characterized by original art forms and unique combinations.

Additional Hardscape Functions

All the other functions—*balance, dimensionality, motion, focal points, delineation of space,* and *outdoor living*—are exemplified in these gardens.

Application

There is no garden that could not benefit from ornamentation through well-placed art objects and sculpted forms. A different style of garden would, of course, require different sorts of objects, but the principle is applicable universally.

Planting

8-26: Hosta 'Chinese Sunrise,' Bergenia *'Alpenglut,'* Brunnera 'Jack Frost,' Hakohachloa 'All Gold,' Cimicifuga 'Black Negligee,' Molina caerulea *'Strahlenquelle.'* At base of right fountain head: Liriope 'Big Blue.' Ground cover: Ophiopogon japonicus 'Nanus'

8-27: (Left to right) Phormium 'Bronze,' in front of that silver plant is *Helichrysum italicum* (Curry Plant), *Geranium* 'Vancouver Centennial' (throughout the mid-ground), *Uncinia uncinata* (copper colored grass), Bergenia *'Alpenglut,' Ophiopogon planiscapus 'Nigrescens,'* Dracunculus vulgaris (aroid with seed forming), *Pennisetum orientale* (grass behind Dracunculus), *Allium cernuum*

8-28: (Background) Miscanthus 'Morning Light,' (left side of pool) Pennisetum 'Hameln,' (right side) Miscanthus 'Hinjo' (Little Nicky)

8-29: Center background conifer is *Cupressus sempivirens* 'Swane's Gold.' Cimicifuga 'Brunette,' Phormium 'Maori Sunrise,' Hebe 'Pluto' (in front of globe), *Thymus serpyllum, Nassella tenuissima,* many different forms of Coleus

A FEW THOUGHTS ON
Making Things

As this garden and other gardens in this book demonstrate, something doesn't have to exist for you to have it. Everything that is made was first conceived and then built, and it can be much easier to have things made or even to make them yourself than most people think. If you have a clear concept for a creation, chances are you can have it made. We don't need to wait for someone else to come up with our dreams. There are countless skilled and helpful people around who will be more than happy to build, out of metal, stone, clay, plastic, wood, or whatever, the object of our dreams and for a reasonable price. The fountains shown in this project, for example, were simply metal tubes taken to an ironworker who cut them to the specified design. The rest was simple installation. In a previous project, you saw a machine especially built to lift heavy stones, and it was a remarkably inexpensive custom creation. Much, much more of this sort of thing can be done than is being done, and all sorts of people are out there willing to help.

Deceptive Depth

S ome gardens are intended to present themselves as pictures—visual scenes meant to be enjoyed solely by the eye and mind **(8-29)**. Characterized by strict control of space and careful use of components, such settings offer little room for accident.

This little garden could be seen as a three-dimensional painting or a piece of sculpted space. Taken as a visual whole, it is entirely an ornament in and of itself. It derives its apparent depth from the clever use of a large mirror behind the statue. The mirror occupies the entire rear wall, so that everything seen in the arch behind the sculpture is a reflection. The geranium seems to flow back, through another arch, behind the sculpture, toward more garden space, upon which French doors look out. In reality, those doors are behind the viewer and there is only the one arch.

Scale/Proportion
The statue, which is the focus of this setting, is less than life-size, so the plantings are likewise reduced. Because we normally see pines much larger than these, the dwarf pines (*Pinus mugo 'Mops'*) set the scale and have the effect of raising the scale of the statue and everything else without making anything appear too large. The box topiary, if larger, would shrink the scene, and if smaller, raise it.

Style
Classically formal.

Additional Hardscape Functions
This garden could have been used in Chapter 5 on *focal points,* and there is considerable *dimensionality* in the scene.

Application
Everything works together in this garden to create the overall effect of classical

8-29
A mirror
enlarges this
classically
formal, highly
ornamental
setting.

formality, so the entire setting, including the adjoining architecture, would need to be appropriate. The use of a mirror requires a specific setting seen from a distinct and controlled vantage point and needs a clearly defined composition to reflect in order to be effective. One possible use is in a passageway or a narrow garden with an end wall that the visitor confronts head-on.

Planting

Geranium x *oxonianum, Pinus mugo 'Mops,'* boxwood topiary

Sonoran Asymmetry

In the last garden, we saw a scene enlarged through the use of a mirror and made ornamental through the carefully controlled use of space and objects. In these next two gardens, we treat constricted spaces—each in an entirely different manner—to make them attractive.

The owners of this newly constructed home in Tucson, Arizona, wanted a beautiful garden, and believed their property to possess the potential, but were unsure of how to develop it (8-30). As this "before" image shows, this was an awkward site of disjointed areas and needed a unifying theme to bring it all together.

Planters in Southwestern-style forms, rhythmically dispersed throughout, would help make sense of the disparate parts—the odd corners and long walls—and with the intermixed paving of beautiful stone and pebbles throughout, would help tie it all together (8-31). They would also add the quality of ornamentation, so dismally lacking in this garden (8-32 and 8-33).

8-30 "Before"—the property much in need of a garden and ornamentation.

8-31 "After"—a series of ornate planters, a water garden, and decorative paving transform the site.

8-32 "Before"—the view from the porch.

8-33 "After"—a much-improved prospect.

8-34 Each planter is of a different size and shape and designed to harmonize with the planters near it.

8-35 View from above.

Although very similar in style, none of the planters is just like any other. They are of different shapes and sizes. Each was designed for its specific place in the garden and to harmonize with the planters near it **(8-34** and **8-35).** The water garden was originally designed as a more compact, three-tiered unit—with the top fountain spilling into the second and third, and the second spilling into the third as well—but this design was altered during construction and is not as it was meant to be.

Scale/Proportion

Though a small space, the garden still has ample room, so the planters seem well scaled within it. However, the water garden should have been about half as long, which would have made the area behind it more gracious.

This is a new garden, so there is too much hardscape to softscape, but that will rectify as the plants mature.

Style

Contemporary Southwestern.

Additional Hardscape Functions

There is a pleasant sense of *motion* created by the interrelations of the planters and the random working of the stone tiles in the pebble bed. The planters also add *dimensionality*.

Application

Small and irregularly shaped areas where planting in the soil is problematic can benefit from this approach. The planters can be of any style suitable for the adjoining architecture.

Planting

Trees: *Acacia* sp., *Bauhinia lunariodes, Chilopsis linearis*

Shrubs: *Asclepias* sp., *Calliandra* x, Dalea, Justicia, Myrtus, *Salvia farinacea, Tecomaria capensis*

Accents: *Agave* sp., *Baileya multiradiata,* Bursera, Calyophus, Erythrina, Euphorbia, Yucca, *Zinnia* sp.

Groundcovers: *Berlandiera lyrata, Bulbine frutescens,* Dalea, Penstemon

Vines: *Rosa banksiae 'Lutea,' Mascagnia macroptera, Maurandya antirrhiniflora*

Italian Landscape
in Tile Murals

Very narrow gardens are among the most difficult to make attractive (8-36). Often, there is hardly enough space for plantings, let alone for objects that add beauty. In such instances, it may be expedient to use the vertical dimension—in this case, the walls of the garden—to bring forth the qualities of ornamentation and beauty (8-37).

This garden is in the shape of an *L* on its back, with the long arm 30 feet in length, the short, 20, and both are only 9 feet wide (8-38 and 8-39). An urban site, this was the only garden space available to these owners and two children, so creating an inviting environment without encroaching on the tiny space was essential.

8-36 The long arm of the *L*, before redesign.

8-37 The long arm of the *L* after, now with hand-painted tile murals framed in individually created wrought-iron arches.

8-38 The short arm of the *L*—"before."

8-39 The corner—"before."

8-40 The garden, toward the short arm of the *L*—"after."

8-41 The corner—"after."

Apart from the containers, which take up room, the only planting areas were the few inches behind the brick wall. The problem was how to create beauty without taking up living space. When looked at in that way, the solution became obvious.

The intent was to create a garden setting without the benefit of a lot of plants. Creating murals surrounding the garden space (**8-40** and **8-41**) would achieve this end. The tile murals are of an Italian landscape rendered abstractly. *Tromp l'oeil* would not have worked here because of the nearness of the murals, though the upper panel of willows blowing through an open window is in a *tromp l'oeil* style.

The scene begins at one end with willow leaves (which pick up the upper mural) flowing down into a country landscape (**8-42**). The country landscape of the central panels blends into cultivated fields that move toward an abstract village scene (**8-43**), and the last panel is of a private garden with a barely recognizable Hydrangea and willow branches. The panel beneath the water garden is of irises (**8-44**).

The murals are framed in wrought-iron arches with ornate iron scrollwork above, holding lanterns arching outward. Smaller, iron-lattice arches separate the panels. Vines grow up these lattice panels, around the arches, and through the scrollwork. The opposite wall, against the house, also has this ornate scrollwork, which terminates in saucers and rings of various sizes for holding pots—out of the way of bodily movement (**8-45**). On the tall rear wall, beneath the willow window and the iris panel, is a lead fountain, as seen above in **8-37**. At the other end of the short arm of the *L* is a fountain at ground level (**8-46**).

All of this created the sense of a highly ornamental garden with minimal planting. Virtually none of the usable space has been taken up, yet there is the feeling of being surrounded by a beautiful garden.

Scale/Proportion

The mural panels definitely dominate the scene, but as they are two-dimensional they are not obtrusive. In fact, they draw us out and expand our sense of space. The panels and the scrollwork on top of them also set a vertical limit, maintaining focus within the garden rather than allowing the surrounding buildings to intrude. Once the vines cover the scrollwork, nearly complete privacy will be achieved.

Style

Art nouveau with classical undercurrents.

8-42 The series of murals ends (or begins) with an abstract garden scene with willow leaves and a Hydrangea.

8-43 The garden changes dramatically in different light.

8-44 The water garden with the panel of irises below.

8-45 The entire garden is irrigated by a drip irrigation system, which waters the beds and each of the pots in their iron saucers or rings.

8-46 The ground-level water fountain consists of five copper "stems," through which water is pumped into leaf-shaped cups, which fill, bob down, drop the water, and bob back up. The fountain was designed this way to bring enjoyment through the window of the below-ground basement room, as well as to the garden.

Additional Hardscape Functions

There are *focal points* (note the two fountains at each end and the mask) and considerable *dimensionality* in the iron framework, which give depth to the murals and a vertical lift.

Application

Tile murals are a vastly underutilized means of ornamentation. They can be of any style, a range of sizes and colors, and used in countless ways to bring brightness and beauty to any garden area. Similarly, wrought iron can greatly enhance many garden styles.

Planting

Between the murals are *Ilex crenata* 'Sky Pencil' and *Clematis* sp. Beneath the willow mural are daylily and Iris, and to their left, *Euonymus japonicus 'Aureomarginata'* and Wisteria. To the right is a willow shrub. In the center corner is a cherry tree (*Prunus* x), and *Daphne* x *burkwoodii 'Carol Mackie,'* Liriope, Ophiopogon, and miniature daylilies are distributed throughout.

Poured Planters

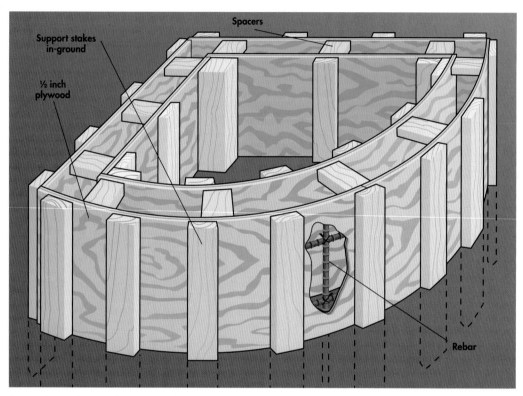

Support stakes
in-ground

Spacers

½ inch
plywood

Rebar

8-47 Curved poured-concrete planter.

The curved poured planter is similar to the poured footing and poured retaining wall in Project 7A on pages 208 to 209, except that plywood is used for the form boards rather than two-by material **(8-47)**. A single piece of ½-inch plywood will permit a considerable curve and can be staked into place and braced, as the illustration shows.

For a thicker curved wall, it may be necessary to double up the plywood, and for extremely sharp bends, two or more ¼-inch pieces of plywood can be used.

Plywood comes in 4-foot by 8-foot sheets and can be cut to the proper height and length. For the footing, excavate to below the frost line, set the forms of cut plywood, and brace

with stakes and spacers screwed into the plywood. For the reinforcing, number three or four rebar can be used, as it is bent easily. For a planter with fairly narrow walls, one piece down the middle is sufficient and as many as are necessary from bottom to top with a distance of 6 to 8 inches between each horizontal length.

It is best to oil the inside of the forms for easy removal. Use one part cement, three parts sand, and five parts gravel, mixed with water into a thick slurry. Fill the forms, banging the sides or plunging a shovel into the cement as you go, to ensure all voids are filled. Once the concrete is hard, the forms can be removed. If necessary, plaster the sides (see Project 7A).

Index

Outdoor-living areas (continued)
  privacy example of, 165
  quiet corner, 192–194
  scale/proportion of examples, 190–191, 192, 196, 198, 206
  styles of examples, 191, 194, 196, 201, 206
  suburban front yard as, 228, 229
  three patios with pool, 202–207
  two rooms and water garden, 188–191
  water gardens and, 188–191, 192–194, 202–207
  with wonderful views, 195–197

P
Pathways. *See* Walks/pathways
Patios
  brick, 198–201
  curved, with rill, 90–93
  free-form, 73, 95
  irregular bluestone, on stone dust project, 97–98
  motion from, 73, 95
  for outdoor-living. *See* Outdoor-living areas
  reflecting pools defining space on, 128–131
  terraced, defining space, 128–131
Paving
  adding warmth, 42
  balance with, 18–21
  defining outdoor-living areas, 187, 188, 192–194
  defining space, 117–122
  formal lawn between, 18–21
  as ornamentation, 219–223, 237
  random, rectangular blue stone on stone dust project, 139

slate, as ornament, 219–223
Pergolas
  defining space, 128
  as focal points, 146
  having purpose, 105
  as ornaments, 222, 223
  privacy with, 162–164
Planters
  as ornaments, 237–241
  poured, project, 248
  privacy from, 175–176
Plantings, of garden examples
  balance, 14, 17, 20
  defining space, 110, 116, 122, 127, 131, 138
  dimensionality, 30, 34, 39, 44, 46, 51
  focal point, 151–152, 156, 157
  motion, 64, 67, 74, 79, 83, 89, 93, 95
  ornamentation, 223, 227, 233, 236, 241, 247
  outdoor-living, 191, 194, 197, 201
  privacy, 165, 168, 170, 172, 174, 176, 179
Pots
  balancing gardens, 8, 9
  as focal points, 150, 157–158
  natural vs. man made elements and, 13
  order of, as ornament, 216–218
  scale/proportion of, 9, 11
  tub garden in, 109, 110
Privacy, 161–179
  arbors for, 179
  balanced garden example of, 24–25
  cedar-on-brick room for, 177–179
  city sanctuary, 175–176
  creating place for, 162–165
  defining space example of, 110
  dimensionality example and, 41

gazebos for, 169–170, 171–172
lattice for, 162, 163, 166–167, 177–179
motion example and, 74
multiple elements creating, 175–176, 177–179
overview, 161
pergola for, 162–164
planters for, 175–176
quiet corner, 192–194
quiet room, 166–168
room by lake, 169–170
rose bushes for, 166–168
scale/proportion of examples, 164–165, 166, 170, 171, 174, 176, 177
styles of examples, 165, 168, 170, 171, 174, 176, 177
tree house for, 173–174
trysting place, 173–174
two rooms and summer house, 177–179
vine roofs for, 177–179
water gardens for, 175–176
Problem sites, 47
Projects
  bluestone walk with Belgium-block risers, 100–101
  brick and lattice garden house, 180–182
  brick walk with mortared outer course, 54–55
  built-in wall fountain, 183–184
  dry-laid stone wall, 56–58
  flexible-liner pond, 141–144
  formal fountain, 159
  fountains, 159, 160, 183–184
  irregular bluestone patio on stone dust, 97–98
  making things and, 233
  poured-concrete retaining wall/footing, 208–209

Credits

Garden Design Credits

Tomasina Beck: 6-4
Susan Birdsall: 3-12 to 3-22, 8-2
Christopher Costin: 6-1
Laura Crockett: 8-23 to 8-28
Keith Davitt: 2-7 to 2-23, 2-26 to 2-31, 2-36, 3-1 to 3-11, 3-23 to 3-48, 3-55 to 3-58, 4-1
    to 4-46, 6-7 to 6-15, 7-4 to 7-7, 7-15 to 7-30, 8-1, 8-3, 8-30 to 8-46
Helen Faulls: 1-13, 1-14
Charles Funke: 5-6
Jim Garland: 8-17 to 8-22
Kerry Mendez: 5-10, 5-11
Dianne Olcott: 5-5, 5-7
Robert Seigal: 1-5, 1-6, 1-8, 1-10, 1-11, 1-12, 1-18, 1-19, 1-20, 1-21, 2-1, 5-1, 5-9, 8-8 to 8-16
Susy Smith: 8-5,
Somerset Tintenhul: 5-4
Alan Titchmarsh: 2-4, 8-29
Nani Waddups: 6-6
Ron Wagner: 6-6
Owners with assistance from Perennial Partners: 3-49 to 3-54

Other Credits

Italian Landscape In Tile Murals: Mural design, Keith Davitt; Mural execution, Isabelle Deloye;
Ironwork design, Keith Davitt; Ironwork fabrication, Architectural Metals

Garden Photography Credits

Keith Davitt: 1-5, 1-6, 1-8, 1-10, 1-11, 1-12, 1-18, 1-19, 1-20, 1-21, 2-1, 2-7 to 2-23, 2-26
    to 2-31, 2-36, 3-1 to 3-58, 4-1 to 4-46, 5-1, 5-5, 5-7, 5-9, 5-10, 5-11, 5-14, 5-15, 6-7
    to 6-15, 7-1 to 7-30, 8-1, 8-2, 8-3, 8-4, 8-8 to 8-22, 8-29, 8-30, 8-36, 8-38, 8-39
Tim Fuller: 8-31, 8-32, 8-33, 8-34, 8-35, 8-41 to 8-45
John Glover: 1-2, 1-4, 1-13, 1-14, 1-15, 1-16, 1-17, 2-4, 2-24, 2-25, 5-4, 5-6, 5-8, 5-12, 6-1,
    6-2, 6-3, 6-4, 6-5, 8-5, 8-6, 8-7
Lucy Hardiman: 8-23 to 8-28
Allan Mandell: 6-6
Curtis Taylor: 8-37, 8-40, 8-46

About the Author

Keith Davitt is a landscape designer/builder, author, and photographer who has built and designed projects nationwide and has had speaking engagements around the country. He has been designing, building, photographing, and writing about gardens for over two decades. He contributes to such magazines as *Fine Gardening, Garden Design, Gardening How-to, Horticulture, Period Homes, Traditional Building, WaterShapes,* and numerous others.

He is frequently asked to teach landscape design in various venues, including botanic gardens; to give presentations and conduct seminars and symposiums; and to appear on television shows.

His published books include *Small Spaces Beautiful Gardens* and *Beyond the Lawn* from Rockport Publishers, and *Water Features for Small Gardens* from Timber Press. He was a major contributor to *Fine Gardening's, Gardening in Small Spaces.*

Keith lives in upstate New York where he conducts ongoing design classes to individuals and small groups. He can be contacted through his Web site, www.gardenviews.com.